SCIENCE AND RELEGION

THE PARADOX OF EXISTENCE: SCIENCE AND RELIGION IN HARMONY

HASEEB JAVED

Made with ♥ on the Notion Press Platform
www.notionpress.com

Dedicated to my teachers who instilled in me a love for knowledge and a passion for exploration. To my political brothers who have always been a source of support and inspiration. To my family and parents who have nurtured and guided me through every step of my life. You have been my rock and I am eternally grateful for all that you have done for me.

Contents

Foreword

Foreword by Ahmed Ali:

It is with great honor and privilege that I write this foreword for Haseeb Javed's latest literary masterpiece. Haseeb, a young and talented writer from the backward village of Azad Kashmir, has truly stunned the world with his exceptional writing skills.

As a reader, I was taken on a journey through the pages of this book and was thoroughly impressed by the depth of knowledge and the passion that Haseeb has for history. His writing style is both informative and engaging, making it a true joy to read.

What is truly remarkable about this book is that it has been written by a young man who, despite the challenges of living in a backward village, has managed to make a name for himself in the literary world. This serves as an inspiration to us all and proves that with hard work, dedication, and perseverance, anything is possible.

My favourite line from the book is: "History has a funny way of repeating itself, and those who don't learn from the past are doomed to repeat it." This line encapsulates the importance of understanding and appreciating our history, a theme that runs throughout the book.

I wholeheartedly recommend this book to anyone who is passionate about history and wants to learn more about the world we live in. Haseeb Javed is a talented writer who has a bright future ahead of him, and I cannot wait to see what he will write next.

Ahmed Ali

Preface

In the world of knowledge, the relationship between Science and Religion has been an ongoing topic of debate and discussion for centuries. "Science and Religion" attempts to shed light on this complex and controversial relationship by exploring its historical roots, contemporary perspectives, and future possibilities.

The purpose of this book is to provide an in-depth examination of the relationship between Science and Religion, highlighting its impact on society, culture, and education. The book is organized into ten chapters that explore a range of topics, including the definition of Science and Religion, their historical relationship, the conflict between them, the perspectives of different religious traditions, the influence of Science and Religion on popular culture and education, and the reflections of prominent figures from different fields.

This book offers a comprehensive and nuanced view of Science and Religion, addressing both their similarities and differences. It provides insights into the historical roots of the relationship, tracing it back to ancient civilizations and their beliefs. The book also sheds light on the scientific revolution and its impact on religion, as well as the influence of religion on scientific discovery and advancement. The conflict between Science and Religion, which has been a major point of contention for centuries, is also explored in depth.

In addition to these historical perspectives, the book also examines the current state of the relationship between Science and Religion in modern society, exploring the role they play in shaping public opinion, ethics and morality, and politics and government. The book also delves into the perspectives of different religious traditions, including a detailed examination of Muslim perspectives on Science and Religion.

The book also explores the role of Science and Religion in popular culture, including their portrayal in books, movies, and TV shows, as well as their impact on pop culture trends and public perception of science. Finally, the book addresses the role of Science and Religion in education, examining their impact on the science curriculum, teacher education, and student attitudes towards science.

This book is a valuable resource for anyone seeking to deepen their understanding of the relationship between Science and Religion. Whether you are a scientist, a religious scholar, a student, or simply someone interested in exploring the intersection of these two important fields, "Science and Religion: Discussing from Start" provides a comprehensive and accessible overview of this complex and fascinating topic.

I hope that this book will inspire further exploration and discussion of the relationship between Science and Religion, and that it will serve as a valuable resource for those seeking to deepen their understanding of this important topic.

Prologue

I. Introduction

- The purpose and goals of the book
- Definition of Science and Religion
- The relationship between Science and Religion

II. Historical Overview of Science and Religion

- Ancient civilizations and their beliefs
- The Scientific Revolution and its impact on Religion
- The role of religion in shaping scientific discovery
- The influence of religion on scientific advancement

III. The Conflict between Science and Religion

- Examples of conflicts between Science and Religion
- The conflict between Science and Religion in the 19th and 20th centuries
- The reasons for the conflict between Science and Religion
- The efforts to reconcile Science and Religion
- The impact of conflicts on society

IV. Science and Religion in Modern Society

- The current state of the relationship between Science and Religion
- The role of Science and Religion in shaping public opinion
- The impact of Science and Religion on ethics and morality
- The influence of science and religion on politics and government

V. Muslim Perspectives on Science and Religion

- The role of Islam in shaping scientific discoveries
- The Islamic view on the relationship between Science and Religion
- The influence of Islam on scientific advancements
- The integration of Islamic beliefs in scientific research

VI. Islamic Thought and Science: A Historical Overview
The Quranic view on Science and Religion
The Islamic Golden Age and its impact on Science and Religion
The Muslim philosophers and scientists who bridged Science and Religion
The role of the mosque in promoting scientific literacy
The contemporary Muslim discourse on Science and Religion
The impact of Science and Religion on the Muslim identity
The role of Science and Religion in shaping Muslim attitudes towards modernity
The relationship between Science and Religion in Muslim-majority countries
The impact of Science and Religion on Muslim-majority societies

The role of Science and Religion in shaping the future of the Muslim world.

VII. Science and Religion in Popular Culture

- The portrayal of Science and Religion in books, movies, and TV shows
- The impact of Science and Religion on pop culture trends
- The role of Science and Religion in shaping public perception of science
- The influence of Science and Religion on the media and journalism
- The role of Science and Religion in shaping the public's understanding of science

VIII. Science and Religion in the Classroom

- The teaching of Science and Religion in schools
- The role of Science and Religion in shaping science education
- The impact of Science and Religion on the science curriculum
- The role of Science and Religion in shaping teacher education and training
- The role of Science and Religion in shaping student attitudes towards science

IX. Quotations and Insights from Famous People and Religious Leaders

- The views of scientists, philosophers, and religious leaders on Science and Religion
- The influence of famous people and religious leaders on shaping our understanding of the relationship between Science and Religion
- Reflections on the future of Science and Religion from prominent figures in different fields

X. Conclusion

- Summary of key points
- Reflection on the journey exploring the relationship between Science and Religion
- Personal reflections from the author on the significance of exploring the relationship between Science and Religion.

CHAPTER ONE

I. Introduction

- **The purpose and goals of the book**

The purpose and goals of the book are to explore and examine the relationship between science and religion, and to understand their interactions and influences on each other. The book seeks to answer questions such as: What is the definition of science and religion? How have they coexisted throughout history? What have been some of the conflicts and efforts to reconcile these two seemingly disparate fields? The book also aims to shed light on the current state of the relationship between science and religion in modern society and the role they play in shaping public opinion, ethics, morality, politics, and government.

Moreover, the book delves into the perspective of one major world religion, Islam, and its views on science and religion. It covers the Islamic view on the relationship between science and religion, its impact on shaping scientific discoveries, the integration of Islamic beliefs in scientific research, and the role of science and religion in shaping Muslim attitudes towards modernity and the future of the Muslim world.

Additionally, the book aims to explore the impact of science and religion on popular culture, including their portrayal in books, movies, and TV shows, and their influence on public perception of science and shaping public understanding of science. The book also discusses the teaching of science and religion in the classroom, including the role they play in shaping science education, the science curriculum, teacher education and training, and student attitudes towards science.

Finally, the book concludes with a summary of key points and reflections on the journey exploring the relationship between science and religion, including insights and reflections from famous people and religious leaders. The author's personal reflections on the significance of exploring this relationship provide a thought-provoking conclusion to this comprehensive and in-depth exploration of science and religion.

- **Definition of Science and Religion**

Science and religion have long been seen as separate entities, but many people find that they can exist in harmony. Science is a systematic exploration of the natural world and its laws, relying on evidence and logical reasoning to form theories and make predictions about physical phenomena. It is often seen as an impartial form of knowledge that forms the basis for much of modern technology and medicine.

Religion, on the other hand, is a set of beliefs, values, and practices that give individuals purpose and meaning. It provides answers to questions regarding life's purpose, the existence of a higher power, and what happens after death. While there are differences between the two, science and religion can be reconciled by recognizing their shared goals: understanding truth and providing guidance for living. This recognition allows them to work together to bring greater insight into our lives and our world.

- **The relationship between Science and Religion**

The relationship between science and religion has been a subject of intense debate and discussion for centuries, with both sides offering compelling arguments in support of their beliefs. Science is seen as a source of empirical knowledge that relies on facts and evidence to explain the world around us. On the other hand, religion provides spiritual guidance and moral insight into our understanding of life's purpose. While some believe that these two fields are complementary sources of knowledge, others argue they can be conflicting forces when it comes to certain issues. Throughout history there have been numerous examples where scientific discoveries have challenged traditional religious teachings or vice versa, leading to heated debates about how best to reconcile the two disciplines. Ultimately, this tension between science and religion exists because each offers different yet equally valid ways of looking at the world, we live in.

The main source of conflict between science and religion lies in their different ways of approaching questions about the world and the universe. Science is based on empirical evidence, which means that it relies upon observation, experimentation, and measurement to form conclusions. The scientific method involves a systematic collection of data followed by an analysis using reason and logic to make conclusions about the natural world. On the other hand, religion relies more heavily on faith than facts; it looks to scripture as well as tradition for answers about life's meaning and purpose. As these two distinct approaches often lead to conflicting beliefs or interpretations of reality, disagreements can arise between science and religion. In some cases, these conflicts can become quite heated as both sides attempt to assert their own understanding over that of the other.

One of the most well-known and longest running conflicts between science and religion is the debate over the theory of evolution. Many religious believers reject the idea that humans evolved from apes, as it contradicts their interpretation of the story of creation in the Bible. However, there has been an overwhelming amount of scientific evidence to support evolutionary theory since its inception more than a century ago, leading to a conflict between science and religion that has yet to be fully resolved. This ongoing tension between two seemingly incompatible worldviews has caused much controversy throughout history as each side seeks to prove its own validity while discrediting opposing views. Despite numerous attempts at reconciliation, this debate continues today with no clear resolution in sight.

Another area of conflict between science and religion is in the field of ethics and morality. While science can provide us with a greater understanding of the world around us, it cannot offer any definitive answers to questions about right or wrong. Religion, however, provides its followers with a moral code that outlines how they should live their lives according to certain spiritual beliefs and ethical principles. This often leads to tension when scientific discoveries or advancements challenge traditional religious values or ethical standards that have been accepted for centuries. As technology continues to advance at an ever-increasing rate, this clash between science and religion will likely remain a source of contention well into the future.

Despite these conflicts, there are also many examples of science and religion working together in a mutually beneficial way. For example, religious leaders and communities have embraced science as a tool for understanding the world around them and improving human life. This has enabled scientific progress to be made with an ethical framework that takes into account moral considerations. Scientists too have recognized the importance of incorporating spiritual or religious perspectives when conducting research. In doing so they can gain greater insights into how their work impacts society on both physical and metaphysical levels. As such, it is possible for science and religion to coexist harmoniously, each offering valuable contributions to our knowledge of the universe we inhabit.

In conclusion, the relationship between science and religion is complex and multifaceted. While there are certainly conflicts between these two fields, it is important to note that in many cases, science and religion have been able to coexist peacefully. In fact, some have argued that both science and religion can be seen as complementary forces which can work together for a greater good. For example, religious institutions often provide funding for scientific research projects or support initiatives aimed at improving public health. Similarly, scientists may use their findings to inform theological debates or spiritual practices. Whether the relationship between science and religion will continue to evolve and improve remains to be seen but it is clear that both science and religion will continue to play an important role in shaping our understanding of the world around us as well as our place within it.

CHAPTER TWO

II. Historical Overview of Science and Religion

- **Ancient civilizations and their beliefs**

The relationship between science and religion has been a topic of discussion for centuries. From ancient civilizations to modern times, the way in which people understand and reconcile the two concepts has changed and evolved over time. In this section, we will delve into the beliefs of ancient civilizations and how they viewed the relationship between science and religion. Ancient civilizations such as the Greeks, Romans, and Egyptians had unique beliefs and understandings of the world around them. The Greeks, for example, believed in a pantheon of gods and goddesses who controlled the natural world and human affairs. Science and religion were intertwined, as the gods were seen as the source of all knowledge. This led to the creation of mythology, which was used to explain natural phenomena and the workings of the world. Similarly, the Egyptians had a complex belief system that included a multitude of gods and goddesses. They believed that the gods controlled the natural world, and their religion was intertwined with science as they believed that the gods were the source of all knowledge. This led to the development of mathematics, astronomy, architecture, engineering, medicine, and more.

The Romans also had a complex belief system that included multiple gods, and they believed that these gods controlled the natural world. The Romans were known for their engineering and technological advancements, which were heavily influenced by their religious beliefs. Religion played a significant role in Roman scientific achievements as they often saw their gods as being responsible for providing knowledge about nature and its workings. Additionally, temples were built throughout Rome dedicated to various gods who were seen as having special powers or knowledge related to different aspects of life.

In conclusion, ancient civilizations viewed the relationship between science and religion in different ways but often saw them as intertwined concepts. These beliefs played an important role in shaping culture during this time period as well as influencing many aspects of scientific progress including mathematics, astronomy, engineering, medicine, architecture, and more.

- **The Scientific Revolution and its impact on Religion**

The Scientific Revolution was a period in the 16th and 17th centuries that saw a profound transformation in the way humans understood the natural world. Prior to this time, the dominant paradigm in Europe was a combination of Aristotelianism and the belief in a static, geocentric universe. This traditional view had been accepted for centuries by both scientists and religious authorities alike, but it soon began to be challenged by an emerging group of thinkers who sought to uncover new truths about nature through observation and experimentation. Prominent figures such as Galileo Galilei, Nicolaus Copernicus, and Johannes Kepler were instrumental in overturning these old ideas with their revolutionary discoveries which revealed that our universe is actually heliocentric rather than geocentric; furthermore, they showed that it is constantly changing rather than being fixed or immutable.

This revolution had far-reaching implications for religion since it called into question the authority of the church which had previously been seen as having absolute control over truth. The Catholic Church maintained that all heavenly bodies revolved around Earth according to scripture; however, when scientific evidence emerged showing otherwise it became clear that its teachings were not infallible after all. As such, this period marked an important shift away from blind faith towards more critical thinking based on empirical evidence.

This led to a period of intense conflict between science and religion, with scientists and philosophers such as Galileo and Giordano Bruno facing persecution from the church for their beliefs. Despite this, however, the ideas of the Scientific Revolution continued to spread throughout Europe and beyond; it was embraced by many who saw it as an opportunity to challenge traditional religious dogma in favor of scientific exploration. This period ultimately resulted in a new way of thinking about the universe which has shaped our understanding ever since - leading to the development of modern science as we know it today. While this period was marked by heated debates and clashes between science and religion, it also sparked critical examination and rethinking of traditional beliefs which continues to be seen in all areas of life even now. It is clear that without this revolutionary time in history, humanity would not have made such incredible advances in pursuit of knowledge over recent centuries.

In conclusion, the Scientific Revolution was an important turning point in human history; it revolutionized our understanding of nature and ushered in a new era of scientific progress. It also helped spark conversations about how we can reconcile faith with reason, as science began to challenge traditional religious beliefs that had been accepted for centuries. This dialogue between science and religion continues today, making the Scientific Revolution an essential part of our ongoing discourse on this topic.

- **The role of religion in shaping scientific discovery**

Religion has had a profound influence on the development of scientific discovery throughout history. In many ancient civilizations, religion and science were inextricably linked and used to explain natural phenomena and comprehend the world around them. For instance, in ancient Greece, astronomy and mathematics were studied as a way to gain insight into the gods and their actions. Similarly, in ancient China Taoist philosophy was an important factor that contributed to advances in science, mathematics, and medicine. These two examples demonstrate how religious beliefs have shaped our understanding of the universe over time.

In medieval Europe, religion was an integral part of life and had a profound effect on scientific discovery. At the time, the Catholic Church held tremendous influence over knowledge and learning. While they supported scientific study as a way to comprehend God's marvelous creation, there were strict boundaries in place that ensured science would not challenge or contradict Biblical teachings. This meant any new discoveries had to be consistent with religious doctrine in order for them to gain acceptance within society. As such, much of what we know about science during this period is heavily influenced by faith-based principles and beliefs.

During the Scientific Revolution of the 16th and 17th centuries, a major shift in thinking occurred which changed the relationship between religion and science. This was due to an increased focus on empirical observation rather than authority-based knowledge, as well as advances in scientific discoveries. As such, traditional religious beliefs were challenged and tension arose between religion and science. Those who embraced this new way of thinking viewed it as an opportunity to gain further insight into God's creation, while others saw it as a threat to their religious authority. Ultimately, this period marked a significant change in how religion and science interacted with each other.

Despite the conflict between religion and science that has existed throughout history, religion has continued to shape scientific discovery in a variety of ways. For example, the works of natural philosophers like Sir Isaac Newton and Robert Boyle were deeply influenced by their religious beliefs; they saw their scientific discoveries as a way to understand the natural laws that God had put in place. Similarly, many scientists today are motivated by their religious beliefs to seek answers to the mysteries of the universe and use their knowledge for good. Through this approach, these scientists strive to make a positive impact on society through research and innovation inspired by faith.

In conclusion, religion has had an undeniable impact on scientific discovery throughout history. While there have been cases in which science and religion have been at odds with each other, religion has also served as a source of inspiration for many scientists and played a role in guiding their inquiry. Even today, religious beliefs continue to influence and motivate the work of numerous scientists; thus, the relationship between science and faith remains an ongoing subject of dialogue and debate.

- **The influence of religion on scientific advancement**

The influence of religion on scientific advancement has been a topic of debate and discussion for centuries. While some view religion as an obstacle to scientific progress, citing its reliance on faith rather than evidence-based research and the potential tension between religious beliefs and scientific theories, others see it as a source of inspiration and motivation. Many scientists point to their own personal religious belief systems as having provided them with the courage needed to pursue groundbreaking discoveries that have advanced humanity's understanding of the natural world. Furthermore, many religions contain values such as respect for nature or dedication to truth which can be seen in how science is practiced today. Ultimately, while there may be disagreement about how much impact religion has had on science over time, it is undeniable that this relationship continues to shape our modern society in various ways.

Religion has had a profound influence on the development of science throughout history. In ancient civilizations such as Greece, China, and India, religion was deeply intertwined with scientific pursuits; many scientists of the time viewed their work as an attempt to uncover the mysteries of both the universe and gods. This led to impressive advancements in mathematics, astronomy, medicine and other fields. For example, in Ancient Greece religious beliefs helped inspire advances in geometry which were then used by astronomers like Ptolemy to accurately map out constellations and planets. Similarly in India's Vedic period there was a strong emphasis placed on astrology which eventually developed into more advanced forms of astronomy over time. These examples demonstrate how religion can be seen as having played a vital role in inspiring scientific progress throughout history.

In the medieval period, religion was a powerful influence on scientific development and discovery. The Church played an influential role in shaping scientific thought by promoting the belief in a flat earth and geocentrism. These ideas were accepted as fact due to religious teachings, but with the Scientific Revolution of the 16th and 17th centuries, science began to challenge traditional religious beliefs. Scientists such as Galileo Galilei were met with opposition from the Church for their discoveries that contradicted long-held religious views. This conflict between religion and science marked a turning point in history, leading to increased acceptance of new scientific theories which would eventually shape our understanding of the world around us today.

However, religion has also had a positive influence on scientific advancement. Many scientists throughout history, including Isaac Newton and Louis Pasteur, have been motivated by their religious beliefs to pursue scientific discovery. Newton, for example, saw his work in physics and mathematics as a way to uncover the laws of nature set forth by God. He believed that by understanding the natural world he could gain insight into how it was designed and created by God - something which would ultimately lead him closer to understanding His mind. Similarly, Pasteur was motivated by his religious beliefs to study the causes of diseases and develop treatments for them; seeing this as an opportunity to serve humanity while fulfilling what he perceived as God's plan or purpose. Both men used science not only as a means of discovering new knowledge but also as a method through which they could get closer to their faith-based ideals.

Today, religion continues to influence scientific advancement, though in a different way than it did in the past. In many cases, religion and science are seen as separate spheres of knowledge, with each having its own purpose and goals. However, some scientists still view their work through a spiritual lens; for them, understanding the mysteries of the universe is an act of exploration that can uncover divine truths about our world. This spiritual motivation continues to drive their work and leads to discoveries that may have otherwise gone unnoticed or unexplored. As such, religion remains an important part of scientific progress even today.

It is also important to note that while the theory of evolution is widely accepted among the scientific community, it is still a theory and not an indisputable fact. Despite its widespread acceptance, there are still ongoing debates and discussions within the scientific community about the specific mechanisms of evolution which have yet to be fully understood. As such, evolutionary biology remains an area of active research with new discoveries being made all the time.

In conclusion, it is evident that the relationship between religion and scientific advancement is a complex one. On one hand, religious beliefs have been known to be an obstacle to progress in certain areas of science; however, on the other hand, many scientists throughout history have drawn inspiration from their faith and used it as a source of motivation for their work. Therefore, while religion can sometimes impede scientific development, its influence can also be positive.

CHAPTER THREE

III. The Conflict between Science and Religion

The conflict between science and religion has been a long-standing debate that has persisted throughout history. This refers to the tensions and disagreements between the two spheres of influence, as they often present different perspectives and beliefs on a wide range of topics. These conflicts can range from fundamental disagreements about the nature of reality, such as whether or not God exists or how life originated, to more specific debates about the morality and ethics of certain scientific practices such as genetic engineering or animal testing. This clash between religious faith and scientific evidence has had an impact on many aspects of society, with some believers rejecting scientific findings in favor of their own spiritual convictions while others attempt to reconcile both disciplines in order to form a unified understanding.

- **Examples of conflicts between Science and Religion**

Examples of conflicts between science and religion include: the debate over evolution versus creationism, the belief in miracles that contradict scientific explanations for natural phenomena, and disputes over whether or not humans have a soul. In addition to these more well-known topics, there are other areas where science and religion disagree such as cosmology (the study of the origin and structure of the universe) which some religious traditions view as being created by God while scientists believe it formed through natural processes. Furthermore, certain moral issues related to medical treatments like abortion or euthanasia can cause disagreement between those who adhere to religious beliefs and those who rely on scientific evidence when making decisions.

Evolution and Creationism:

One of the most well-known conflicts between science and religion is the debate over the theory of evolution and the belief in creationism. Evolution, as presented by Charles Darwin, states that species evolve and change over time through a process of natural selection. This means that organisms with advantageous traits are more likely to survive and reproduce than those without them, leading to gradual changes within a population over generations. Meanwhile, creationism posits that God created the world and all living creatures as they are today, which implies no evolutionary change has taken place throughout history. These two theories have been at odds for centuries due to their conflicting views on how life came into being; however, recent discoveries in genetics have provided some evidence that both sides may be partially correct.

The Big Bang Theory and Creationism:

Another major conflict between science and religion is the debate over the Big Bang theory and belief in creationism. The Big Bang theory states that the universe began as a single, infinitely dense point of matter known as a singularity which has been expanding ever since. On the other hand, creationism holds to the notion that God created everything on Earth in six literal days as described in Genesis. This fundamental disagreement between science and religion has caused much contention throughout history, with both sides passionately defending their respective positions.

Stem Cell Research and Ethics:

The debate between science and religion over stem cell research has been ongoing for many years. Some religious groups believe that life begins at conception, and therefore they consider embryonic stem cell research to be immoral and unethical. However, a number of scientists have argued that this type of research could lead to major breakthroughs in the field of medicine, with potential treatments available for a range of diseases or conditions. Despite these differences in opinion, both sides agree on one thing: more research is needed into the ethical implications before any decision can be made about how it should be used.

Climate Change and Environmental Issues:

Climate change and environmental issues have been a source of tension between science and religion for some time. Many religious groups view environmental degradation as the result of human sinfulness and greed, while scientists point to the overwhelming evidence of human-caused climate change as well as its potential devastating effects on our planet if we do not take action to address it. This difference in opinion has caused an ongoing debate between those who believe that humans are responsible for their actions and those who believe that God is ultimately in control. Ultimately, both sides must come together to find solutions to this global problem before it is too late.

These conflicts between science and religion can have a profound effect on society, causing divisions that may manifest in tensions between different groups. This discord can also impede the advancement of scientific knowledge, as certain areas of research may be discouraged or even prohibited due to religious opposition. Nevertheless, despite these clashes between science and religion, there are still efforts underway to bridge the gap between them and create an environment where they can coexist peacefully. Such initiatives seek to find common ground where both sides can come together in mutual understanding and respect in order to promote progress for all.

- **The conflict between Science and Religion in the 19th and 20th centuries**

The conflict between Science and Religion in the 19th and 20th centuries was a significant event in the history of the relationship between science and religion. During this time, the scientific community had made immense progress with discoveries such as Darwin's theory of evolution, Einstein's Theory of Relativity, and advances in medicine that challenged traditional religious beliefs. This led to a great deal of tension between those who held on to their faith-based beliefs, and those who believed that science could offer better explanations for how our world works. The debate over whether or not scientific theories should be accepted as fact or dismissed due to its potential threat to established religious doctrine became increasingly heated throughout this period. Ultimately, it resulted in a greater understanding from both sides about how science can work alongside faith without necessarily contradicting one another.

One of the most significant and memorable examples of this conflict between science and religion was when Charles Darwin published his famous work "On the Origin of Species" in 1859. This book presented a revolutionary theory that all living things had evolved over time, rather than being created by God as many religions believed. As expected, this idea caused an immense amount of controversy among religious leaders and communities who saw it as a direct attack on their beliefs. They were unwilling to accept such a radical concept which contradicted traditional teachings about creationism.

The Scopes Trial of 1925 was a major example of the conflict between science and religion in the 19th and 20th centuries. This trial, which took place in Tennessee, USA, focused on whether or not it was legal to teach evolution in public schools. It was seen as a significant test of how much influence religion had over scientific education at that time. The outcome of the trial set an important precedent for future generations; it showed that religious beliefs should not be imposed onto scientific education and instead allowed students to make up their own minds about what they believe is true. Furthermore, this decision had far-reaching implications for the relationship between science and religion; it highlighted that there must be mutual respect between both sides if we are to progress scientifically without infringing on anyone's right to practice their faith freely.

In addition to these high-profile conflicts, there were numerous other examples of tension between science and religion during this period. One such example was the controversy over eugenics, which sought to improve the genetic quality of a population through selective breeding. This raised questions about the ethical implications of intervening in nature and challenged religious beliefs that viewed humans as divinely created beings. Similarly, stem cell research and advances in reproductive technologies presented moral dilemmas due to their potential for manipulating life at its most fundamental levels. These conflicts reflected not only a clash between scientific progress and traditional religious views but also highlighted how profoundly science was impacting society's overall understanding of faith.

Despite these conflicts, many religious leaders and communities were able to reconcile their beliefs with the advancements of science. They did this by engaging in open dialogue and actively seeking to understand each other's perspective. This helped to ease some of the tension between the two domains, as it enabled them to find a way to coexist and continue to shape each other's development. By being willing to compromise and meet halfway on certain issues, both religion and science could move forward together rather than remain at odds with one another. Ultimately, this mutual understanding has been beneficial for both fields of study as they have been able to learn from each other's ideas while still maintaining their own distinct identities.

- **The reasons for the conflict between Science and Religion**

The conflict between Science and Religion has been a complex issue for centuries, with roots dating back to ancient times. This tension has affected many aspects of life throughout history and is still present today. The clash between the two spheres of knowledge and belief has been shaped by a variety of factors, such as changes in society, culture, technology advances, political ideologies, economic systems and social movements. It is not only an ideological debate but also a practical one; different scientific theories have challenged accepted religious beliefs while some religions have sought to control or limit scientific progress. In recent years there has even been an increase in dialogue between science and religion as both sides attempt to understand each other better. Despite the differences that remain between them, it seems likely that this discourse will continue into the future as both science and religion seek to reconcile their respective ways of interpreting the world around us.

One of the key reasons for the conflict between Science and Religion is the differing methodologies used to understand the world. Science relies heavily on empirical evidence and logical reasoning, utilizing experimentation, observation, and data analysis in order to draw conclusions about our universe. On the other hand, religion often relies on faith and tradition that has been passed down through generations; beliefs that are not necessarily based on scientific proof or research. When these two worldviews collide, it can lead to misunderstandings, misinterpretations, and disagreements as each side attempts to defend their own interpretation of reality.

Another reason for the conflict between Science and Religion is that science often challenges religious beliefs and practices. For example, the theory of evolution suggests that species evolve over time through natural selection, which contradicts the idea of creationism or intelligent design that is central to many religious beliefs. This challenge has caused a great deal of tension between the two worldviews as religion seeks to provide an explanation for how life came into being while science looks to empirical evidence to explain what it observes in nature. Additionally, the discovery of other planets and the idea of the Big Bang theory have challenged traditional religious views of the universe and our place within it. These discoveries have forced people who adhere to certain religions to re-examine their faith in light of new scientific evidence about how life began and how old our planet truly is. The clash between these two different ways of understanding reality can be quite intense at times, but ultimately serves as a reminder that both perspectives are important parts of human history and culture.

Moreover, political and cultural factors have also played a role in shaping the conflict between Science and Religion. During the 19th and 20th centuries, for example, many Western societies were undergoing significant changes in terms of politics and social structures. This was characterized by increasing secularization as well as greater emphasis on individual rights, which clashed with traditional religious beliefs that had previously dominated society. As a result, Science and religion were often pitted against each other as competing ideologies, with each seen as representing a different aspect of society. This further fueled the conflict between the two; while some argued for their compatibility others saw them as fundamentally incompatible worldviews leading to debates and controversies that continue to shape the relationship between Science and Religion to this day.

In conclusion, the conflict between Science and Religion is a complex and multifaceted issue that has been shaped by a variety of factors. These include different methodologies used to understand the world, challenges to traditional religious beliefs, political and cultural influences, and more. Despite these conflicts, there have also been attempts throughout history to reconcile Science and Religion in order to find common ground between them. This includes initiatives such as interdisciplinary dialogue between scientists and theologians or interpretations of Scripture that are compatible with scientific evidence. Ultimately, it is clear that this ongoing debate will remain an important part of our understanding of both science and religion for years to come.

- **The efforts to reconcile Science and Religion**

The efforts to reconcile Science and Religion have been a long-standing issue throughout history, with many religious groups rejecting scientific discoveries that conflict with their beliefs. This has caused tension between the two for centuries, as science continually advances and changes our understanding of the world around us. In response to this, some religious groups have sought to find a harmonious relationship between faith and science. During the 19th and 20th centuries in particular, there were numerous attempts made by various individuals and organizations to bridge the gap between religion and science. These included initiatives such as developing new interpretations of scripture which incorporate modern scientific knowledge, or reinterpreting certain religious doctrines in light of recent scientific discoveries. As society's reliance on technology has grown over time due to rapid advancements in science, so too have these efforts become increasingly important in order for both sides to coexist peacefully.

One of the earliest efforts to reconcile Science and Religion was made by the German philosopher Immanuel Kant. Kant was a devout Christian, and he sought to find a way to bridge the divide between science and religion in order to create an environment where both could coexist harmoniously. He believed that both science and religion were essential components of human understanding, with each providing valuable insight into our world – but they should not conflict or compete against one another. Instead, he argued that science and religion should be seen as complementary forces; working together for mutual benefit rather than being at odds with one another.

Another notable effort to reconcile science and religion was made by the American philosopher William James. James, a psychologist and philosopher, argued that both science and religion were important to human understanding, but that they should not be in conflict with each other. He believed that science was concerned with studying the physical world while religion focused on exploring the spiritual realm. To this end, he proposed that it was possible for science and religion to coexist peacefully as two distinct bodies of knowledge; one dealing with facts about the natural universe while the other explored moral values or faith-based beliefs. Ultimately, he sought to create an atmosphere where both disciplines could be respected without either side having to compromise their fundamental beliefs or principles.

In the late 19th century, the Anglican clergyman and scientist John Henry Newman sought to bridge the gap between Science and Religion. He believed that science was essential for understanding physical phenomena, but that religion was necessary for comprehending spiritual matters. He argued that both science and religion were required in order to gain a full appreciation of reality. For Newman, scientific knowledge provided an insight into how the world worked on an empirical level while religious faith illuminated our understanding of morality, purpose and meaning. His attempt to reconcile these two seemingly disparate fields resulted in a holistic view of truth which encompassed both scientific fact and spiritual belief.

Throughout the 20th century, there were numerous other efforts to reconcile Science and Religion. These attempts at reconciliation ranged from the philosophical musings of Teilhard de Chardin, who believed that science and religion could work together to understand the evolution of the universe, to more practical steps taken by religious institutions like the Roman Catholic Church. The latter was particularly noteworthy in its attempt at bridging this divide following Galileo's famous confrontation with church authorities over his heliocentric model of our Solar System. This episode highlighted a need for greater collaboration between science and religion if they were ever going to come together as equals in understanding how we fit into this vast universe. As such, it is no surprise that many prominent figures throughout history have sought ways to bring these two fields closer together - something which has become increasingly important as scientific progress continues apace.

In recent years, there has been a concerted effort to bridge the gap between Science and Religion in order to better address the global environmental crisis. This is especially true in fields such as ecology and environmentalism, where religious leaders have argued that science and religion must work together if we are to successfully tackle the pressing issues of climate change, resource depletion, ocean acidification and other forms of ecological degradation. By combining their respective expertise on these matters - scientific knowledge with spiritual insight - it is hoped that more effective solutions can be developed for dealing with this urgent challenge.

In conclusion, it is clear that throughout history there have been a number of attempts to reconcile Science and Religion. Some of these efforts have had positive results, while others have not achieved the desired outcome. Nevertheless, the goal of finding a harmonious relationship between the two remains an important issue in today's world. People from all walks of life continue to search for ways to bridge this gap and find common ground between scientific fact and spiritual truth. It is hoped that with continued effort we can eventually find harmony between these seemingly disparate fields so that both science and religion may be respected equally by our society.

- **The impact of conflicts on society**

The impact of the conflicts between science and religion on society has been significant and far-reaching. Throughout history, the relationship between science and religion has been marked by tensions and debates, with each side vying for dominance and influence. This conflict is often seen as a battle between two competing worldviews: one that sees faith as an essential part of life, while the other sees scientific evidence as its primary source of truth. The struggle between these two perspectives has had a profound effect on how people view their place in the universe and their relationship to God.

The conflict between science and religion has been particularly intense in the 19th and 20th centuries, when scientific discoveries challenged long-held religious beliefs about creationism, evolution, cosmology, geology, astronomy, physics etc., leading some to reject traditional religious teachings altogether. This period also saw a dramatic shift away from established religious authority towards more secular forms of knowledge such as philosophy or psychology – sparking what many refer to as a new era of secularization. As this debate continues today it remains clear that both sides have much to contribute to our understanding of ourselves and our world – even if they don't always agree on how best to do so!

One of the most significant impacts of the conflict between science and religion has been on the way people think about and understand the world around them. The rise of scientific rationalism, which emphasizes evidence-based reasoning and logical thinking to arrive at conclusions, as well as skepticism towards traditional religious beliefs, has changed how individuals view their place in nature. This shift away from a reliance on religious authority has had profound implications for society; it affects everything from an individual's self-perception, to their understanding of the universe, all the way down to how they form social and political structures. In many ways, this clash between science and religion created a new age in human thought that continues to shape our lives today.

The conflict between science and religion has had a profound effect on the way knowledge is generated and transmitted. The scientific method, which relies on empirical evidence and logical reasoning, has challenged traditional religious ways of knowing by offering an alternative approach to acquiring knowledge. This shift towards the scientific method has become increasingly prominent in many parts of the world, leading to a greater emphasis on scientific literacy. Consequently, public policy and decision-making are now often informed by data from scientific studies or research projects rather than relying solely on faith or belief systems. As such, it can be said that science has come to dominate much of our modern understanding of how we acquire knowledge about our world.

Another impact of the conflict between science and religion has been on the way people engage with moral and ethical issues. Scientific advances have challenged traditional religious views on a range of topics, such as abortion, contraception, and same-sex marriage. This has led to passionate debates in which both sides attempt to use scientific evidence to support their claims. In addition, these conflicts have resulted in political polarization as different factions seek to impose their beliefs through legislation or other means. Despite this tension between science and religion, it is also true that this conflict has allowed for a greater appreciation for the role of science in informing moral and ethical decision-making. It is now more widely accepted that there needs to be a nuanced understanding of the relationship between science and religion rather than an absolute dichotomy between them.

Finally, the conflict between science and religion has had a profound impact on the way people practice and understand their faith. For many, science has become a source of spiritual enlightenment in addition to providing an understanding of how things work. This newfound knowledge can be seen as a new source of spiritual inspiration and meaning for those who are open to it. Conversely, for others this tension between science and religion has been too much to bear, leading them to reject religious beliefs altogether. Lastly, there have been some individuals whose response to this conflict was not one of complete rejection but rather a re-examination of traditional religious beliefs; they strive for harmony by taking into account both scientific evidence as well as theological teachings when forming their worldviews, resulting in a more nuanced approach to the relationship between science and religion.

Overall, the impact of the conflict between science and religion on society has been complex and multifaceted. While it has led to significant challenges, such as a mistrust of scientific findings among certain religious groups and an increased politicization of scientific research, it has also sparked constructive dialogue about how both science and religion can coexist in our modern world. This discourse has allowed for a deeper understanding of the relationship between science and religion, encouraging people from different backgrounds to come together to explore new ways that faith and scientific inquiry can work together. As a result, this ongoing debate has opened up opportunities for discovery that span multiple disciplines.

CHAPTER FOUR

IV. Science and Religion in Modern Society

- **The current state of the relationship between Science and Religion**

The relationship between science and religion in modern society is complex. It varies greatly depending on the culture, region, and community one resides in. In some parts of the world, there are areas where both domains overlap and co-exist peacefully. This can be seen through shared values such as environmental stewardship or a reverence for life. On the other hand, there are also places where conflict exists due to differences in beliefs regarding certain scientific theories or religious doctrines. Despite this tension, it remains true that science and religion have been intertwined throughout history and continue to influence each other today in many ways - from how people view their place within nature to how they interpret ethical issues like abortion or euthanasia. Ultimately, it can be said that the two domains continue to have both areas of overlap and areas of conflict in modern society.

On one hand, there are those who see science and religion as inherently incompatible and at odds with each other. They point to conflicts such as the creationism vs. evolution debate, which pits religious beliefs about how life began against scientific evidence that suggests a different timeline of events, and the conflict between certain religious beliefs and scientific discoveries like the age of the Earth, which suggest that our planet is far older than many religions state in their teachings. These issues serve as strong evidence for some people that science and religion cannot coexist peacefully together.

On the other hand, there are those who see science and religion as complementary and believe that they can both coexist and even support each other. They point to the history of science, which is intertwined with religious beliefs; many important scientific discoveries have been made by individuals of faith. For example, medieval monk Gregor Mendel is known as the "father of genetics" for his groundbreaking work in heredity. He was a devout Catholic who believed in both God's laws governing nature and his own ability to understand them through careful observation. Similarly, modern scientists such as Francis Collins continue to embrace their faith while making significant contributions to our understanding of biology. By recognizing that science and religion can be compatible forces for good, we open up new possibilities for exploration into both realms.

Additionally, there are those who take a more nuanced view, recognizing that while some aspects of science and religion may conflict in certain ways, there is also much that they share in common. For example, both science and religion seek to understand the world around us and our place in it - seeking answers to questions about why we exist and what our purpose here on Earth is. Both can provide a sense of comfort or assurance by providing an explanation for life's events; offering hope for the future or helping us make sense of difficult times. In this way, both science and religion can offer meaning and purpose to our lives.

In conclusion, the relationship between science and religion in modern society is complex, multifaceted, and ever-evolving. It can be difficult to reconcile the two, as there are often conflicting views and interpretations of each. However, it's important to remember that there are also areas of commonality and cooperation between them. Ultimately, the relationship between science and religion is shaped by a variety of factors including individual beliefs and values, communities' attitudes towards both topics, as well as wider cultural influences such as education systems or media coverage. As time progresses so too does this dynamic relationship - sometimes for better or worse - but ultimately it remains an integral part of life today.

- **The role of Science and Religion in shaping public opinion**

Science and religion both have the potential to shape public opinion, and the relationship between the two can impact the way people view certain topics and issues. Science often informs public opinion through the advancement of new technologies, such as medical breakthroughs or advancements in renewable energy sources, as well as through research that uncovers new scientific knowledge. Religion shape's public opinion by providing moral guidance on a range of social, ethical, and political issues; it also offers a sense of community for those who share similar beliefs. In this way, religious institutions serve an important role in influencing how individuals think about various topics within society. Ultimately, science and religion are intertwined forces that contribute to shaping our collective understanding of important matters like health care reform or environmental protection initiatives.

In modern society, the relationship between science and religion can be complex and multifaceted. Some individuals view them as completely separate spheres, while others see them as complementary aspects that can work together in harmony. Unfortunately, religious beliefs sometimes come into conflict with scientific findings which leads to public debates and controversies. This is especially evident in recent years with issues such as the teaching of evolution in schools and climate change being hotly contested topics that have highlighted potential clashes between science and religion. In some cases, these differences of opinion have caused heated arguments among members of different faiths – demonstrating how this issue has become a significant source of disagreement in today's world.

On the other hand, some people believe that science and religion can coexist peacefully, and that both can offer valuable insights into the world. This viewpoint is based on an understanding of both disciplines as sources of knowledge which complement each other. For example, scientific research provides a better understanding of the natural world - how it works and why things happen - while religious teachings provide insight into spiritual matters such as morality, ethics, purpose in life and our relationship with God.

In recent years, many religious leaders have sought to bridge this divide by emphasizing that science offers essential tools for exploring physical reality while religion provides a moral compass to guide human behavior. They argue that these two perspectives are not mutually exclusive; rather they should be embraced together in order to promote greater harmony between faith and reason. Furthermore, many organizations have been established with the goal of reconciling science and religion in order to foster public discourse around important issues such as climate change or health care reform. Ultimately, this perspective seeks to emphasize that both science and religion have important roles to play in shaping public opinion and in promoting human progress.

- **The impact of Science and Religion on ethics and morality**

The impact of Science and Religion on ethics and morality has been a topic of discussion and debate for centuries. Science, with its focus on empirical evidence and reason, has challenged traditional religious beliefs and moral codes which were often based upon divine revelation or long-held traditions. Meanwhile, religion, with its reliance on scriptures as well as teachings passed down through the generations, has often resisted scientific advancements that conflict with its doctrines. This tension between science and faith can be seen in many areas such as evolutionary theory or even medical advances involving stem cell research; both sides have passionate advocates who are willing to defend their views vigorously. Despite this clash of worldviews however, there is still much common ground between them; after all, both disciplines seek to promote understanding about the world we live in while also striving to foster a sense of ethical behavior among humanity at large.

Throughout history, various religious traditions have had a huge impact on the values and morals of societies. They have served as a source of ethical guidance for individuals and communities alike. For instance, the Ten Commandments in Judaism and Christianity, the Five Pillars of Islam, and the Four Noble Truths in Buddhism are all examples that have provided moral structure to their respective groups. However, with scientific advancements increasing our understanding of the world around us, some religious leaders and communities have found it difficult to reconcile science with their traditional beliefs or codes of conduct. This has posed an interesting challenge for those who wish to uphold both faith-based teachings and newer discoveries from scientific research.

The 19th and 20th centuries marked a dramatic shift in the relationship between science and religion, as scientific discoveries began to challenge many long-held religious beliefs. This was particularly evident in the fields of biology, geology, and astronomy. A major milestone in this transition was the publication of Charles Darwin's "The Origin of Species" in 1859 which put forth his theory of evolution by natural selection. This directly challenged creationism and the belief that Earth is only a few thousand years old - two ideas that were previously accepted without question by many religious leaders. These new theories sparked heated debates among scientists and religious figures alike, with some arguing for coexistence while others insisted on one or the other being right or wrong.

Despite these conflicts, many religious leaders and communities have sought to reconcile science and religion by finding common ground and integrating scientific discoveries into their beliefs. For instance, some have argued that science can provide an empirical perspective on the world while religion offers a spiritual one, allowing both approaches to complement each other in providing different insights into the same questions. Others have gone further in seeking to integrate scientific knowledge into their religious teachings as a way of deepening understanding of the natural world. In this way, they are able to combine traditional faith-based views with modern scientific thought for a more holistic approach towards comprehending reality.

In recent years, the relationship between science and religion has become increasingly complex. On one side of the spectrum, there are those who advocate for a complete separation between the two disciplines; on the other hand, some continue to seek a harmonious relationship where both can coexist peacefully. This ongoing tension is further compounded by their role in shaping public opinion on ethical and moral issues such as climate change, abortion, same-gender marriage and many others. These topics have been discussed fervently among religious leaders and scientists alike, with no clear resolution in sight. As debates surrounding these matters persist and evolve over time, it remains to be seen how this dynamic relationship will play out in society's collective consciousness moving forward.

Ultimately, the impact of science and religion on ethics and morality is multifaceted. It is shaped by a wide range of factors, including individual beliefs, cultural traditions, and historical contexts. While these two forces may sometimes conflict with one another, they can also be complementary in nature. For example, science can provide us with an understanding of how certain ethical decisions may have consequences that we would not have considered before; similarly, religious teachings often emphasize moral principles that guide our behavior in society. By combining both scientific knowledge and spiritual wisdom together into a holistic approach to life and morality, we are able to gain a deeper understanding of our world and the ethical questions that shape our lives.

- **The influence of science and religion on politics and government**

Science and religion have had a tremendous impact on politics and government throughout history, particularly in terms of the way they shape public opinion and influence decision-making. By providing frameworks for understanding the world around us, both science and religion have been instrumental in forming political systems, creating governance structures, and determining how laws are made. For example, religious beliefs often provide moral guidance that can be used to inform legislation or policy decisions; likewise scientific discoveries may lead to new ways of thinking about social issues or help create more effective systems of governance. As such, it is clear that science and religion continue to play an important role in shaping our societies today.

One of the earliest examples of the influence of science and religion on politics and government can be seen in ancient Greece. In this society, religion and philosophy were closely intertwined, with religious beliefs informing philosophical thought, and vice versa. Many of the most influential philosophers in ancient Greece such as Socrates, Plato, and Aristotle were also religious leaders who used their knowledge to develop theories about ethics, morality and governance that had a profound impact on political structures throughout the region. These thinkers sought to integrate spiritual values into social systems which ultimately shaped much of Greek culture for centuries afterwards. Their ideas continue to resonate today as we explore ways to bring together different belief systems within our own societies.

Similarly, in the medieval period, religion had a pervasive influence on politics and government. In many societies, the church was seen as an all-powerful institution that held sway over laws, policies and even wars. This period also saw the rise of religious authorities who wielded immense political power - such as the papacy within the Catholic Church. The papacy was able to shape public opinion through its control of spiritual matters and by issuing decrees from Rome that were binding upon all believers across Europe. As a result, religious institutions became integral parts of society during this era; their decisions often having far-reaching implications for how people lived their lives and interacted with one another.

During the Enlightenment, science had a profound effect on politics and government. New scientific discoveries and technological advances provided an entirely new framework for political systems to be built upon. This prompted many of the leading philosophers of the time to consider how these principles could be applied in their theories of government. John Locke was one such philosopher who embraced this approach, believing that governments should be based on empirical evidence and rationality - concepts derived from the scientific method. He argued that any laws or regulations passed by a government should have a basis in rational thought, rather than dogma or tradition.

In modern times, the relationship between science and religion has become increasingly complex in terms of their influence on politics and government. In some cases, religious beliefs have been seen as threatened by scientific progress and this has led to attempts from religious institutions to limit the impact of science on political decisions. Conversely, there are many societies in which science and religion are viewed as two sides of the same coin. In these scenarios, religious leaders often use scientific evidence to support their views when engaging in political discourse or making decisions that affect governmental policy. As such, it is evident that the influence of both science and religion on politics and government can vary significantly depending upon context.

Regardless of the specific context, it is clear that science and religion have had an immense impact on politics and government throughout history. They have provided moral and ethical guidance to societies, shaped public opinion through religious texts or scientific discoveries, and influenced decision-making at all levels of society. This influence can be seen in many aspects of political life such as laws, regulations, policies, education systems etc. As a result, it is important to understand the relationship between science and religion when studying the political and social history of any society in order to gain a better understanding of how these two forces interact with one another in shaping our world today.

CHAPTER FIVE

V. Muslim Perspectives on Science and Religion

- **The role of Islam in shaping scientific discoveries**

The role of Islam in shaping scientific discoveries is an important one, as it has had a major impact on the development of science and scientific thought throughout history. Islamic culture has been instrumental in advancing scientific knowledge, making key discoveries in areas such as mathematics, astronomy and medicine. This is due to the fact that the Islamic faith promotes an environment that encourages intellectual inquiry and fosters curiosity for its own sake. For example, during the medieval period, Muslim scholars were responsible for translating ancient Greek texts into Arabic which allowed their ideas to spread further than ever before. Furthermore, they made many original contributions to various fields by building upon existing knowledge while also introducing new concepts or theories. This resulted in significant advancements being made across multiple disciplines which have shaped our understanding of science today.

One of the key ways in which Islam has shaped scientific discoveries is through its emphasis on seeking knowledge and understanding. In Islam, the pursuit of knowledge is seen as a religious duty, with an emphasis on critical thinking and inquiry. This approach to learning has been fundamental in creating a culture that encourages exploration and innovation. The Islamic Golden Age (8th-14th centuries) was an era of remarkable intellectual advancement, where scholars, scientists and philosophers produced groundbreaking works across many disciplines such as medicine, astronomy and mathematics. During this period there were significant advances made in areas like algebraic geometry, surgery techniques, optics and pharmacology - all thanks to the Islamic belief that studying nature was part of worshipping God. This legacy continues today with Muslims around the world making valuable contributions to science from fields ranging from physics to engineering.

Another way in which Islam has shaped scientific discoveries is through its view of the natural world. In Islam, the natural world is seen as a manifestation of God's will and as a source of revelation about the nature of the divine. This understanding has led to an appreciation for all forms of life, and encouraged scientists and philosophers to seek a deeper understanding of the natural world. As such, this philosophical approach has been fundamental in driving important breakthroughs in fields such as astronomy and medicine throughout Islamic history. For example, many advances were made during medieval times when Muslim scholars sought to understand how celestial bodies moved across space or how plants could be used for medicinal purposes. By looking at nature from an Islamic perspective – one that sees it both as an expression of God's power and beauty – these scientists were able to make incredible discoveries that have influenced modern science today.

Furthermore, Islamic scholars and theologians have been instrumental in bridging the gap between science and religion. They have provided philosophical and theological frameworks which allow us to better understand how the two interact with one another. Notable Muslim philosophers such as Al-Farabi and Ibn Rushd (also known as Averroes) developed influential ideas about the relationship between reason and revelation, exploring how philosophy can shape our understanding of the world around us. These theories continue to be studied today for their timeless insights into human knowledge.

In conclusion, it is clear that the role of Islam in shaping scientific discoveries has been significant. Through its emphasis on seeking knowledge and understanding, its view of the natural world, and its philosophical and theological frameworks for understanding the relationship between science and religion, Islam has provided an important platform for fostering a culture of inquiry and critical thinking. This has encouraged not only discovery but also the pursuit of knowledge for its own sake. As such, it can be argued that Islam's contribution to scientific progress throughout history cannot be understated; indeed, Islamic scholars have made great strides in advancing our collective scientific knowledge over many centuries.

- **The Islamic view on the relationship between Science and Religion**

From an Islamic perspective, there is a belief that science and religion are complementary and not in conflict with each other. Islam recognizes the importance of both seeking knowledge and having faith, understanding that they can work together to help us better appreciate God's power and wisdom. In fact, seeking knowledge is considered a religious duty in Islam, as stated in the Qur'an: "And say: My Lord! Increase me in knowledge." (Qur'an 20:114). This emphasis on learning has been further emphasized by Islamic tradition which promotes the idea of using scientific inquiry to gain greater insight into the natural world around us as a means of deepening our appreciation for God's handiwork. By exploring nature through scientific lenses, we are able to see more clearly how powerful and wise God truly is.

The Islamic view of the relationship between science and religion is one of harmonious coexistence, where scientific discoveries and advancements can be seen as a way to deepen one's understanding and appreciation of the world around them, while also recognizing the divine wisdom behind it. Islam does not reject or condemn scientific discovery, but rather encourages it as a means for improving the lives of people, bettering society, and deepening our understanding of God's creation. Muslims believe that by exploring science we can gain further insight into God's grand design for humanity - an endeavor which should be pursued with enthusiasm in order to uncover new aspects about His power and might.

In practice, this means that Muslims are encouraged to engage in scientific inquiry and discovery with the understanding that such knowledge should be used ethically and morally. Science is not viewed as an end unto itself, but rather something to be utilized for the betterment of humanity and its well-being. In doing so, it is expected that Muslims will use their scientific knowledge in accordance with principles of justice, compassion, fairness and the greater good. This allows science to become a powerful tool for social progress while ensuring ethical boundaries are maintained.

Thus, the Islamic view on the relationship between science and religion is one of mutual reinforcement. Science can help to deepen an individual's faith by providing evidence for God's creations, while religious teachings provide a moral and ethical framework for how scientific knowledge should be used responsibly. This intertwining of science and religion helps to create a holistic understanding of life that allows individuals to achieve spiritual fulfillment through their exploration of scientific truths.

- **The influence of Islam on scientific advancements**

The influence of Islam on scientific advancements is a complex topic that has been studied and debated for centuries. Islam, like other religions, has had a profound impact on the development of science throughout history. Islamic scholars have contributed greatly to many areas of scientific inquiry such as mathematics, astronomy, medicine, chemistry and physics. The Islamic view on the relationship between science and religion is unique in comparison to other faiths; this is largely due to its strong emphasis on reason and rational thought which was embraced by many early Muslim thinkers. Moreover, the cultural norms surrounding education in many Islamic societies also encouraged scientific exploration and discovery. Furthermore, historical events such as the fall of Baghdad's House of Wisdom in 1258 CE have also played an important role in shaping how Muslims perceive their relationship with science today.

One of the most significant ways in which Islam has influenced scientific advancements is through its promotion of scientific inquiry and education. The Islamic faith places great emphasis on the pursuit of knowledge and understanding, encouraging Muslims to explore their surroundings and gain insight into how things work. This focus on learning has been reflected in the establishment of institutions of higher learning, such as madrasas, across the Islamic world. These educational establishments have been instrumental in advancing the study of science, providing resources for students to become knowledgeable about a range of subjects from mathematics to philosophy. As a result, some of history's greatest Muslim scientists, mathematicians and philosophers have emerged from these institutions over time.

Islam's view of the natural world has been a major influence on scientific advancements throughout history. Islamic teachings emphasize that God created the universe and all its components, and this creation reflects His divine order and wisdom. This idea has inspired Muslim scientists to explore the natural world in an effort to gain further insight into the workings of God, leading them to make significant discoveries over time. By studying nature, they have uncovered invaluable knowledge about how things work, which has served as a foundation for many modern-day inventions and innovations. As such, it can be said that Islam's reverence for nature has had far-reaching implications for scientific progress throughout history.

Overall, Islam has played a major role in the development of scientific advancements throughout history. Its view of the relationship between science and religion is one that encourages exploration and discovery, believing that these two areas are not mutually exclusive but rather complementary to each other. This important ideology has been influential in stimulating modern scientific inquiry and discovery; it encourages individuals to explore their environment with an open mind while also staying true to their religious beliefs. As such, its influence can be seen today as scientists continue to make advances in various fields across the globe.

- **The integration of Islamic beliefs in scientific research**

Islamic beliefs and values have had a profound effect on the way scientific research has been conducted in Muslim-majority societies. For example, Islamic scholars have long emphasized the importance of humility and seeking knowledge as a means to deepen one's understanding of God. This emphasis has encouraged curiosity about the natural world, an appreciation for its complexity and beauty, as well as a respect for Nature itself. It is these same values that have driven Muslim scientists to explore various aspects of science with passion and dedication over centuries - from mathematics to medicine, astronomy to engineering – all in pursuit of greater knowledge and wisdom. As such, we can see how Islamic beliefs and values have shaped not only our understanding of science but also the way it is practiced today.

In addition, Islamic beliefs about the nature of the universe and the role of humanity have had a profound impact on scientific research. Muslim scientists have been motivated by their faith to explore and understand God's creation, believing that it is part of their sacred duty as humans to do so. This belief has pushed them to delve into the mysteries of science in order to uncover its secrets and use this knowledge for good, such as helping improve people's lives through medical advancements or providing clean energy sources. The Islamic view that humans should strive towards understanding and improving our world has inspired generations of Muslim scientists who have made incredible contributions to our collective knowledge.

Overall, the integration of Islamic beliefs into scientific research has been hugely beneficial to the development of scientific knowledge. Muslim scientists have made invaluable contributions to fields such as astronomy, medicine, mathematics and physics, helping us gain a deeper understanding of our universe and our place within it. This integration has helped shape the direction of scientific inquiry in many ways - from providing an ethical framework for conducting experiments and interpreting results to inspiring new ideas that would not have otherwise come about without this influence. Through their work, Muslim scientists have had a lasting positive impact on science as we know it today.

CHAPTER SIX

VI. Islamic Thought and Science: A Historical Overview

- **The Quranic view on Science and Religion**

Understood, here's an extended version that incorporates more verses and provides a more in-depth understanding of the Quranic view on Science and Religion:

The Quranic view on Science and Religion is one of harmony and complementarity. The Quran recognizes the importance of scientific inquiry and encourages its followers to seek knowledge and understand the workings of the natural world. At the same time, it also stresses the importance of faith and the role that religion plays in shaping our understanding of the world.

One of the key verses that highlights the importance of scientific inquiry in Islam is verse 2:282, which states: "O you who have believed, when you contract a debt for a specified term, write it down. And let a scribe write [it] between you in justice. Let no scribe refuse to write as Allah has taught him. So let him write and let the one who has the obligation dictate. And let him fear Allah, his Lord, and not leave anything out of it. But if the one who has the obligation is of limited understanding or weak or unable to dictate himself, then let his guardian dictate in justice."

This verse lays out the importance of documenting and recording scientific knowledge and serves as an encouragement to seek and acquire knowledge. The Quran also recognizes the value of science in helping us understand the natural world, as demonstrated in verse 16:12, which states: "And He has subjected to you, from Himself, all that is in the heavens and all that is on the earth; it is all as a favor and kindness from Him. Verily, in this are signs for a people who reflect."

In addition to these verses, the Quran also acknowledges the limitations of human understanding and encourages its followers to remain humble in their pursuit of knowledge. For example, verse 6:59 states: "With Him are the keys of the unseen; none knows them but He. And He knows what is in the land and the sea; not a leaf falls but he knows it. And there is not a grain in the darkness of the earth nor anything green nor dry but it is written in a clear record."

This verse highlights the idea that there is much that we do not know and that there are aspects of the world that are beyond our understanding. It serves as a reminder to remain humble in our pursuit of knowledge and to acknowledge that there may be limits to what we can understand through science alone.

verse 2:164, which says, "In the creation of the heavens and the earth, and the alternation of night and day, there are indeed signs for those of understanding." This verse highlights the idea that the natural world provides evidence of the existence and greatness of God. It also emphasizes the importance of using reason and understanding to reflect on the signs in creation, and to develop a deeper appreciation for the wisdom and power of the Creator.

In Islam, the pursuit of scientific knowledge is seen as a form of worship and a way of fulfilling one's duty to seek knowledge and understand the signs of God in the world. This view encourages Muslims to engage in scientific inquiry and to seek a deeper understanding of the natural world. At the same time, it recognizes that ultimate truth and understanding can only come through the revelations of God, as represented in the Quran and other sacred texts. The Quranic view on science and religion is therefore one of complementarity and integration, rather than conflict or competition.

Overall, the Quranic view on Science and Religion is one of complementarity, where both are seen as important tools for understanding the world around us. The Quran recognizes the value of scientific inquiry and encourages its followers to seek knowledge and understand the workings of the natural world, while at the same time stressing the importance of faith and humility in our pursuit of knowledge.

- **The Islamic Golden Age and its impact on Science and Religion**

The Islamic Golden Age was a time of great intellectual and cultural growth in the Islamic world, spanning from the 8th to the 14th century. During this period, Muslim scholars and scientists made remarkable contributions to many fields of knowledge. In mathematics, for example, they developed algebraic equations and advanced trigonometric functions; in medicine they established hospitals and wrote comprehensive medical textbooks; in astronomy they identified constellations and recorded accurate observations about planetary motion; while in philosophy they debated complex metaphysical questions. These advancements helped shape the course of science and religion in the Islamic world as well as having an enormous impact on subsequent developments in knowledge and culture across Europe, Africa, Asia, and beyond.

One of the most remarkable accomplishments of the Islamic Golden Age was the establishment of a structured system for learning and research. This provided an opportunity for scholars to pursue their intellectual interests, as well as share their knowledge with others. Universities and libraries were built in order to facilitate these activities, becoming hubs where students could learn from knowledgeable teachers, debate ideas among peers, and explore new theories. As a result of this institutionalized system of education, science and religion flourished during this period; it enabled people to gain valuable insights into both disciplines that would have otherwise been impossible.

The impact of the Islamic Golden Age on science and religion cannot be overstated. During this period, many scientific discoveries and innovations were based on Islamic principles and beliefs. Muslim scholars of that time believed that knowledge should be pursued as a religious duty, viewing science as an avenue to gain a better understanding not only of our world but also of the divine. This integration between faith and reason helped to create a vibrant intellectual culture in which scientific inquiry was seen as being in harmony with religious devotion rather than conflicting with it. As such, the legacy left by this era is still felt today in various aspects of both science and religion.

In addition to its impact on science and religion, the Islamic Golden Age also had a lasting effect on the world as a whole. During this period, Muslim scholars and scientists made significant advances in various fields such as mathematics, astronomy, medicine, chemistry and philosophy. Their works were instrumental in laying the foundations for many of the intellectual developments that would take place during later centuries. The discoveries of Muslim scientists and philosophers served to shape European science and philosophy significantly; their ideas helped to form much of what is now known as modern Western thought today. As a result, it can be said that without these achievements made during the Islamic Golden Age, our understanding of scientific principles may have been drastically different than it is today.

- **The Muslim philosophers and scientists who bridged Science and Religion**

Throughout history, there have been many Muslim philosophers and scientists who have made significant contributions to both science and religion and who have sought to reconcile the two. Some of them are;

Abu Nasr Al-Farabi (872 – 950)

Also known as Alpharabius. Arab scientist and philosopher, considered as one of the preeminent thinkers of medieval era.

Al-Battani (858 – 929)

Also known as Albatenius. Arab mathematician, scientists and astronomer who improved existing values for the length of the year and of the seasons.

Ibn Sina (980 – 1037)

Also known as Avicenna. Persian philosopher and scientist known for his contributions to Aristotelian philosophy and medicine.

Ibn Battuta (1304 – 1369)

Also known as Shams ad–Din. Arab traveler and scholar who wrote one of the most famous travel books in history, the Rihlah.

Ibn Rushd (1126 – 1198)

Also known as Averroes. Arab philosopher and scholar who produced a series of summaries and commentaries on most of Aristotle's works and on Plato's Republic.

Muhammad ibn Musa Al-Khwarizmi (780 – 850)

Also known as Algoritmi or Algaurizin. His works introduced Hindu-Arabic numerals and the concepts of algebra into European mathematics.

Omar Khayyam (1048 – 1131)

Persian mathematician, astronomer, and poet, known for his scientific achievements and Rubaiyat ("quatrains").

Thabit ibn Qurra (826 – 901)

Also known as Thebit. Arab mathematician, physician and astronomer; who was the first reformer of the Ptolemaic system and the founder of statics.

Abu Bakr Al-Razi (865 – 925)

Also known as Rhazes. Persian alchemist and philosopher, who was one of the greatest physicians in history.

Jabir Ibn Haiyan (722 – 804)

Also known as Geber. The father of Arab chemistry known for his highly influential works on alchemy and metallurgy.

Ibn Ishaq Al-Kindi (801 – 873)

Also known as Alkindus. Arab philosopher and scientist, who is known as the first of the Muslim peripatetic philosophers.

Ibn Al-Haytham (965 – 1040)

Also known as Alhazen. Arab astronomer and mathematician known for his important contributions to the principles of optics and the use of scientific experiments.

Ibn Zuhr (1091 – 1161)

Also known as Avenzoar. Arab physician and surgeon, known for his influential book Al-Taisir Fil-Mudawat Wal-Tadbeer (Book of Simplification Concerning Therapeutics and Diet).

Ibn Khaldun (1332 – 1406)

Arab historiographer and historian who developed one of the earliest nonreligious philosophies of history. Often considered as one of the forerunners of modern historiography, sociology and economics.

Ibn Al-Baitar (1197 – 1248)

Arab scientist, botanist and physician who systematically recorded the discoveries made by Islamic physicians in the Middle Ages.

And many more Muslim philosophers and scientists not only made important contributions to their respective fields, but also helped to bridge the gap between science and religion, and their influence can still be seen today. [Have a look at few of them at the end of book]

It is important to note that while some Muslim philosophers and scientists sought to reconcile science and religion, others believed that the two were inherently in conflict and that science was a threat to religious beliefs. Nevertheless, the contributions of Muslim philosophers and scientists to both science and religion have been significant, and they continue to shape our understanding of the relationship between the two.

- **The role of the mosque in promoting scientific literacy**

The role of the mosque in promoting scientific literacy is an important aspect to consider in the relationship between Science and Religion, especially in the Muslim world. Historically, the mosque has served as a center of learning and knowledge, providing education to people of all ages and backgrounds. The mosque was not only a place of worship, but also a place where people could come to learn about a wide range of subjects. This included science-related topics such as mathematics, astronomy, chemistry, physics and engineering; these studies were often facilitated by professional scholars who taught at mosques across various regions. In addition to this formal instruction provided by experts on these topics, many Muslims had access to informal educational opportunities through discussions with friends or family members about scientific ideas or concepts that would be discussed during sermons at the local mosque. As such, it can be seen that mosques have historically played an important role in advancing scientific literacy among Muslims throughout history.

During the Golden Age of Islam, mosques were incredibly important in promoting scientific literacy and advancing knowledge. Mosques provided an environment where Muslim philosophers and scientists could share their ideas, collaborate on research projects, and make significant contributions to the field of science. This was supported by Caliph Al-Mamun of Baghdad who established a scientific center attached to a mosque known as the "House of Wisdom". This center became renowned for its role in encouraging scientific inquiry and research from scholars all over the world. Scientists would come to this center to study, exchange ideas, discuss theories, and present their findings with others. It was here that some of the most groundbreaking discoveries in science were made during this period.

Today, many mosques around the world continue to promote scientific literacy in a variety of ways. For example, there are programs in place that provide science education to children and young people through the mosque, such as hands-on experiments, lectures, and interactive workshops. This helps to foster a love of learning and appreciation for science among those who attend these events. By emphasizing the role of the mosque in promoting scientific literacy it also highlights the compatibility between Science and Religion; showing that they can work together harmoniously to advance knowledge and understanding. Through this approach people gain an appreciation for how both Science and Religion have something important to offer when it comes to developing our understanding of the world, we live in.

- **The contemporary Muslim discourse on Science and Religion**

The contemporary Muslim discourse on Science and Religion has been shaped by a rich and diverse history of philosophical and scientific thought, as well as contemporary debates and discussions about the role of religion in shaping societal norms and values. Historically, Muslim philosophers such as Al-Farabi, Al-Kindi, Ibn Sina (also known as Avicenna), Ibn Khaldun, Nasir al-Din Tusi, Mulla Sadra Shirazi have made significant contributions to various fields of science ranging from mathematics to astronomy. Furthermore, renowned Islamic scholars such as Ibn Rushd (also known as Averroes) were known for their efforts to reconcile science and religion through works like The Incoherence of the Philosophers. These pioneering figures sought to integrate scientific knowledge into their religious beliefs and practices while also attempting to bridge traditional Islamic theology with philosophy.

One of the key elements of the contemporary Muslim discourse on Science and Religion is the emphasis on their compatibility and complementarity. In this view, science and religion should not be seen as being in opposition to one another, but rather as two distinct but complementary sources of knowledge. Many contemporary Muslim scholars and thinkers argue that both science and religion can offer valuable insights into understanding our world, with each providing a different yet equally important perspective. This belief is rooted in an appreciation for the fact that both science and religion serve as important sources of truth; while they may come at things from different angles or draw upon different types of evidence, it is possible for them to inform each other's conclusions if approached with an open mind. As such, this discourse seeks to emphasize how these two spheres can coexist harmoniously when understood properly.

The mosque has been an integral part of the Islamic tradition since its inception, and it has played a critical role in promoting scientific literacy among Muslims. During the Islamic Golden Age, mosques served as hubs for learning and intellectual exploration. Scholars and students from all walks of life gathered at these places to share ideas, engage in debates and discussions, and further their understanding of science, religion, philosophy and other fields of knowledge. Mosques were also important centers for preserving ancient texts on mathematics, astronomy, medicine and engineering - providing future generations with invaluable resources that would have otherwise been lost. In this way mosques provided a platform for leaps forward in human progress by helping to spread new discoveries throughout the Muslim world.

Despite this history of reconciliation and collaboration between science and religion, contemporary debates and discussions about the relationship between these two spheres of knowledge can still be contentious. This is especially true in light of recent scientific and technological advancements, such as advances in genetics and biotechnology, that have challenged traditional religious beliefs and practices. Nevertheless, there has been a resurgence of interest among Muslim scholars to re-examine the relationship between Science & Religion from an Islamic perspective. This contemporary Muslim discourse on Science & Religion remains a vibrant dialogue that continues to shape the relationship between these two spheres of knowledge by exploring their intersection points as well as their interdependence upon one another.

- **The impact of Science and Religion on the Muslim identity**

The impact of Science and Religion on the Muslim identity is a complex and nuanced topic that has been the subject of much debate and discussion in the contemporary Muslim world. For many Muslims, their identity is intricately intertwined with their faith in Islam, which provides meaning to their lives and guides them through moral dilemmas. It also shapes how they interact with society by providing an ethical framework for living life in accordance with Islamic teachings. This traditional understanding of Muslim identity requires the existence of a Muslim state in which Islam is the dominant religion and political system, as well as being socially accepted by wider society. As such, it can be seen as rooted deeply into a connection to Islamic beliefs and practices, which are believed to provide a comprehensive way of life that promotes good morals, values and virtues. Thus, science and religion play an important role in helping shape this sense of self-identity among Muslims today; allowing them to find equilibrium between modern scientific discoveries while embracing ancient spiritual beliefs at once.

One of the key ways in which Science and Religion intersect in the Muslim world is in the relationship between the mosque and the promotion of scientific literacy. Historically, mosques have served as a central hub for learning, knowledge, and exploration; not only were they places to worship but also centers for philosophical inquiry and scientific discovery. This was especially true during medieval times when renowned Muslim philosophers such as Al-Farabi, Ibn Rushd (also known as Averroes), and Ibn Sina (also known as Avicenna) made remarkable contributions to various fields including philosophy, medicine, mathematics - all while successfully bridging this gap between Science and Religion. These men are widely recognized today for their accomplishments that helped shape our understanding of these two disciplines.

In the contemporary Muslim discourse, there are a variety of opinions on the relationship between Science and Religion. Some argue that they can coexist harmoniously while others emphasize their fundamental incompatibility. Despite this disagreement, there is a general recognition of the importance of science in advancing knowledge and human understanding. As such, many Muslims strive to find ways to reconcile these two seemingly disparate worldviews by promoting a more holistic view of reality. This often involves an exploration into both scientific discoveries as well as religious teachings in order to gain insight into how science and religion can be seen as complementary rather than contradictory forces in our lives.

For some Muslims, the impact of Science and Religion on their identity is seen as a positive and transformative experience that helps to foster an appreciation for the complexities of life. Through this lens, these individuals are able to gain a deeper understanding of their faith and how it relates to the world around them. For others however, the relationship between Science and Religion can be a source of tension and conflict. These individuals may feel that scientific discoveries challenge traditional teachings within Islam or threaten their sense of identity and belonging in regards to their faith. Regardless, both sides recognize that science has had an undeniable influence on Muslim culture over time, making it difficult for many people to ignore its presence in shaping who they are today.

In conclusion, the impact of Science and Religion on the Muslim identity is complex and multifaceted. Muslims have a wide range of attitudes, beliefs, and cultural practices that are shaped by their engagement with both Science and Religion. While there is a general recognition among Muslims of the importance of scientific progress in advancing knowledge and human understanding, there is also an ongoing commitment to finding ways to reconcile faith with science in order to promote a more holistic outlook on life. This has resulted in many innovative approaches being developed over time which seek to integrate scientific research into Islamic thought while still respecting its spiritual core values. Ultimately, this integration serves as an important reminder for all individuals that no matter how far our scientific discoveries take us, we must always remember the deeper spiritual truths that form our foundation as human beings.

- **The role of Science and Religion in shaping Muslim attitudes towards modernity**

The role of Science and Religion in shaping Muslim attitudes towards modernity has been a complex and multifaceted issue throughout history. During the golden age of Islam, from the 8th to the 14th centuries, Muslims were at the forefront of scientific advancements, making significant contributions to fields such as mathematics, astronomy, medicine, and chemistry. This period saw Muslim scholars exploring ways to better understand their faith through science; they viewed knowledge acquired through scientific study as an opportunity to gain insight into God's divine plan for humanity. The integration of religious beliefs with scientific inquiry allowed them to develop an understanding that there was no conflict between science and religion - instead both could be used together in harmony as tools for deepening one's understanding of godliness.

One of the most notable Muslim philosophers and scientists who bridged science and religion was Al-Farabi. He believed that knowledge of the natural world was essential in order to understand the divine, as it allowed us to gain insight into how God created our universe. Studying the natural world was a form of worship for Al-Farabi, as he saw it as an act of reverence towards God's work. Another famous Muslim scientist who shared this view was Alhazen, who made important contributions to the fields of optics and scientific methodology. His research focused on understanding how physical phenomena worked in order to gain insight into how God had crafted nature through his divine power. He viewed science not only as a means by which we could better comprehend our environment but also an opportunity for spiritual growth; with every discovery came a deeper understanding of both reality and divinity.

The role of the mosque in promoting scientific literacy was highly influential in shaping Muslim attitudes towards science and religion. Mosques were often seen as hubs for learning, where scholars gathered to share their knowledge on a range of scientific and philosophical topics. Students would flock to these mosques to learn about the latest discoveries in science, which helped shape their understanding of both science and religion. This fusion between faith and empirical reasoning provided an important foundation for Islamic thought over many centuries.

However, as the Muslim world encountered colonialism and modernization in the 19th and 20th centuries, attitudes towards science and religion began to shift. Some Muslims reacted with apprehension to these changes, feeling that their traditional way of life was being threatened by Western ideas, and saw modernity as a challenge to their religious beliefs. Other Muslims chose instead to embrace the scientific and technological advancements of the West; they attempted to reconcile science and religion in new ways that allowed them to retain both Islamic traditions while also adapting to the changing times. This process has continued into our own era, with many modern-day Muslims seeking a balance between faithfulness to their heritage while still engaging with contemporary culture.

Today, the relationship between science and religion in the Muslim world is complex and varied. In some countries, there has been a resurgence of traditionalist views that reject any conflict between science and faith. However, in other places, there are those who believe that it is impossible to reconcile religious beliefs with scientific discoveries. This debate over how much influence each should have on modern Muslim culture continues to be an important topic of discussion within the Islamic community today. No matter what side of this divide one may fall on, it cannot be denied that both science and religion play a crucial role in shaping contemporary Muslim attitudes towards modernity.

- **The relationship between Science and Religion in Muslim-majority countries**

The relationship between Science and Religion in Muslim-majority countries has varied throughout history, reflecting the dynamic and evolving nature of both Science and Religion as well as the unique cultural and political context of each country. During the medieval period, Muslim-majority countries were at the forefront of scientific discovery and innovation. In particular, they made significant contributions to fields such as mathematics, medicine, chemistry, astronomy, physics and engineering. This was due largely to their commitment to encouraging intellectual pursuits within Islamic theological frameworks. The works of renowned scholars like Ibn Sina (Avicenna), Al-Khwarizmi (father of algebra) or Al-Razi (Rhazes), among many others are still widely studied today. Their achievements laid down a strong foundation for scientific inquiry that is still evident in modern times.

In the modern era, however, some Muslim-majority countries have experienced tensions between Science and Religion. Conflicting interpretations of Islamic teachings and the role of religion in society have led to debates about the place of science in education, research, and public policy. These debates are often centered around topics such as evolution being taught in schools, religious beliefs influencing medical practices, or how science and technology can be used for economic and political development. In many cases these discussions are highly contested due to differences in opinion between various stakeholders on whether scientific progress should take precedence over religious values or vice versa. As a result, there is an ongoing dialogue within certain Muslim-majority societies that seeks to reconcile faith with scientific innovation so that both can coexist harmoniously.

Despite these challenges, there are also efforts underway in Muslim-majority countries to promote a harmonious relationship between Science and Religion. For instance, some Muslim scholars and educators are working to develop a more nuanced understanding of the relationship between science and religion that recognizes their complementary nature. This includes emphasizing how scientific knowledge can be used as an aid for interpreting religious scripture, while acknowledging that certain topics may be beyond the scope of scientific inquiry. Additionally, there are initiatives underway to promote scientific literacy among students by increasing access to resources such as textbooks and laboratories. Moreover, organizations have been established with the goal of encouraging young people to pursue careers in science and technology through mentorship programs, scholarships, internships and other forms of support.

Overall, the relationship between Science and Religion in Muslim-majority countries is complex and multifaceted. This reflects the diverse perspectives, cultural traditions, and historical experiences of each country. In some countries there may be a tension between scientific progress and religious beliefs or practices. But there is also a general recognition of the importance of balancing scientific discovery with spiritual and ethical values, as well as promoting a harmonious relationship between Science and Religion. Different interpretations abound among Muslims on how to achieve this balance, but they all agree that it must be done in order to ensure both science and religion can thrive without one eclipsing the other.

- **The impact of Science and Religion on Muslim-majority societies**

The impact of Science and Religion on Muslim-majority societies is a complex and multifaceted phenomenon. It refers to the ways in which both science and religion influence and shape the attitudes, beliefs, and behaviors of people in societies where the majority of the population is Muslim. Science has had an undeniable effect on all aspects of life in these societies, from advances in medicine to technological innovation. At the same time, religion has been a source of moral guidance for many Muslims throughout history. The two have often intersected with each other in meaningful ways; for example, Islamic medical texts drew heavily upon scientific research when developing treatments for disease. Furthermore, religious teachings have served as inspiration for some great scientific discoveries made by Muslims over centuries past. In this way, science and religion are two of the most powerful forces in shaping human thought, behavior, and culture—and they have both had a profound impact on Muslim-majority societies throughout history up until today.

Throughout history, science has played a major role in shaping the way that Muslims have understood and interacted with the world. From the earliest days of Islamic civilization, Muslim scientists, philosophers, and theologians sought to integrate scientific knowledge with religious understanding in order to arrive at a comprehensive view of the world. This integration was based on their belief that God had created an orderly universe which could be studied through observation and experimentation. Some of the most famous examples of this integration of science and religion include the works of Al-Haytham, Al-Razi, Al-Battani, and Al-Farabi - all influential Muslim thinkers who sought to bridge the gap between science and religion by combining empirical evidence with theological insights. These scholars were responsible for some major advancements in fields such as astronomy, mathematics, medicine, physics and philosophy; they also helped shape how later generations would approach questions about faith within an increasingly secular society.

In modern times, the relationship between science and religion has become a source of tension and conflict in many Muslim-majority societies. On the one hand, there are those who believe that science and religion are incompatible, viewing scientific knowledge as superior to religious beliefs. They argue that science is the only path to understanding the world and should be given precedence over faith-based teachings. On the other hand, there are those who believe that science and religion can coexist in a complementary manner, with each providing insight into different aspects of reality. These individuals argue that by combining both scientific facts with spiritual truths we can gain a deeper and more nuanced understanding of our world than either could provide alone. In this way they seek to bridge the divide between faith-based traditions on one side, while embracing advances in technology on the other side.

Despite the fact that tensions and conflicts have sometimes arisen between religious beliefs and scientific research, many Muslim-majority societies boast a long history of scientific literacy. This is evidenced by their ongoing contributions to the field of science today. It's clear that religion influences science in multiple ways; for example, religious beliefs and practices can shape how people within these societies view science, as well as be used to support or reinforce those same beliefs. Even though there may be times when it appears that faith and facts are at odds with one another, it is important to recognize the role of religious values in fostering an appreciation for scientific inquiry.

In conclusion, the relationship between science and religion in Muslim-majority societies is highly complex and varied. It has been shaped by a multitude of historical, cultural, and social factors that have resulted in both conflicts as well as collaboration between the two forces. In many cases, this cooperation has had a profound impact on the development of these societies and their views towards modernity. The interplay between science and religion can be seen in areas such as education systems, legal reforms, economic growth strategies, health care initiatives, technological advances etc., all of which have helped to shape Muslim-majority societies into what they are today.

- **The role of Science and Religion in shaping the future of the Muslim world.**

The relationship between Science and Religion has been a complex and dynamic one throughout history, with the two often seen as being in opposition to each other. In the modern Muslim world, this relationship is still fraught with tension. At the heart of this relationship lies an important question: how can science be reconciled with religious beliefs and values that shape individual identity and collective culture? This is a difficult question to answer, especially when it comes to reconciling scientific facts with deeply held spiritual beliefs. It requires careful consideration of both sides of the debate in order to find common ground between them. Ultimately, however, it is essential for people from different cultures and backgrounds to work together towards understanding each other's perspectives so that we may all benefit from advances in science without compromising our faith or traditions.

The impact of science and religion on the Muslim world is a topic of ongoing debate, and one that has important implications for the future of Muslim societies. On one hand, science has played a crucial role in shaping the intellectual, technological, and economic development of Muslim-majority countries. It has provided new insights into how to understand physical phenomena such as gravity or electricity; it has enabled advances in communication technology which have connected people around the globe; it has facilitated medical breakthroughs which have saved countless lives; and it has given rise to economic opportunities that have allowed many countries to become self-sufficient. The practical applications of science are far reaching, offering solutions to a wide range of social and economic problems that affect Muslims all over the world. As such, its influence on modern day Islamic culture cannot be denied.

On the other hand, religion continues to play a central and highly influential role in forming the cultural, political, and moral values of Muslim societies. This has led to tensions between those who prioritize scientific knowledge over religious faith as well as between different strands of Islamic thought that have contrasting perspectives on how science should be utilized in society. Such differences can manifest themselves in debates over issues such as gender equality, freedom of speech and expression, LGBT rights and more - with each side attempting to justify their stance through either scientific or religious reasoning. As a result, we are left with an increasingly complex picture where the boundaries between science and faith become ever blurred.

Despite these tensions, many in the Muslim world see the relationship between science and religion as being mutually beneficial. For instance, some suggest that scientific inquiry can help to strengthen one's faith by deepening their understanding of religious concepts. Additionally, they argue that this process can provide a framework for testing and refining beliefs which may otherwise be taken on faith alone. Furthermore, it could be argued that scientific knowledge can lead to an appreciation of God's work in creating the universe and all its complexity. Ultimately, adherents of Islam believe that both science and religion should be used together to gain a greater understanding of life and our place within it.

As the Muslim world continues to grapple with the challenges of modernity and globalization, the role of science and religion in shaping the future of Muslim societies will remain an important area of study and discussion. Science has been a cornerstone for progress throughout history, providing humanity with invaluable knowledge that has enabled us to advance our understanding of ourselves and our environment. At the same time, religious values have provided a moral framework within which people can live together peacefully. In this context, some see the continued growth of science and technology as an opportunity for the Muslim world to reclaim its historical legacy as a center of learning and innovation while others believe that without adherence to Islamic principles such advancements could lead to further social inequality or even oppression. Consequently, they argue that cultural and moral values enshrined in Islam are essential for ensuring a just and equitable society in years ahead.

Regardless of one's perspective on the relationship between science and religion, it is clear that this relationship will play a critical role in shaping the future of the Muslim world. The two have long been intertwined throughout history, with Islamic scholars making significant contributions to mathematics, astronomy and other scientific fields. In modern times, however, there has been an increased focus on how these two forces interact and how they can be reconciled within societies. Whether this interaction will be characterized by cooperation or conflict - or something in between - remains to be seen but it is likely to be a defining issue for Muslim societies in the years to come. It could shape policy decisions related to education and health care as well as determine which technologies are embraced or opposed within these communities. As such, understanding the complex dynamics at play here is essential if we are to effectively navigate our collective future.

CHAPTER SEVEN

VII. Science and Religion in Popular Culture

- **The portrayal of Science and Religion in books, movies, and TV shows**

The portrayal of Science and Religion in popular culture has been a topic of discussion and debate for many years. In books, movies, and TV shows, Science and Religion have often been depicted as opposing forces that are inherently incompatible. This representation is frequently used to convey the idea that science is rational while religion is based on faith or superstition. However, there are also examples where these two topics are presented in a more reconciliatory light; depicting them as complementary rather than mutually exclusive concepts. These depictions can help to foster an understanding between people with different beliefs by showing how both science and religion can be respected without one being seen as superior to the other. Ultimately, it's up to viewers to determine how they interpret these representations of Science and Religion in popular culture media.

In the past, many works of fiction have depicted Science and Religion as diametrically opposed to one another. Science was often portrayed as a beacon of reason and progress while Religion was presented as an antiquated belief system rooted in superstition. This dichotomy between the two fields was especially prevalent during the Enlightenment and Victorian eras when prominent thinkers sought to discredit traditional religious beliefs by emphasizing scientific advancements. These authors suggested that religion had become obsolete in light of modern science's ability to explain natural phenomena without relying on supernatural forces or explanations. Consequently, this period saw a dramatic shift away from faith-based thinking towards rationalism, with some even going so far as to suggest that science could provide all the answers humanity needed for understanding existence.

In recent decades, there has been a noticeable shift away from the traditional conflict-based portrayal of Science and Religion in literature. Instead, this relationship is now often depicted as one of mutual respect and cooperation between the two disciplines. This new depiction serves to highlight how both Science and Religion can complement each other's perspectives, informing each other in important ways. This newfound complexity in their representation reflects a more nuanced understanding of the relationship between Science and Religion that has emerged over time.

For example, some popular works of fiction, such as the science-fiction series Star Trek and Doctor Who, have explored the ways in which Science and Religion can coexist and interact. In these shows, characters often struggle to reconcile their scientific knowledge with their spiritual beliefs. This is an important topic for viewers to consider because it raises questions about how our beliefs shape our understanding of reality. Through debates and discussions between characters on various topics like the nature of existence and morality, these shows encourage us to think critically about our own views on life's big questions.

Additionally, there has been an increase in works of fiction that focus specifically on the intersection of Science and Religion. For example, the novel "The Da Vinci Code" by Dan Brown explores the idea of a secret society that seeks to protect the ancient knowledge and wisdom of the world's great religions, while also incorporating elements of science and technology. This novel is based around a quest for answers about life's biggest questions using both scientific and spiritual methods. It examines how these two seemingly disparate concepts can actually be complementary when viewed from different perspectives. The story follows protagonist Robert Langdon as he unravels hidden secrets and discovers truths about humanity's past which challenge his beliefs about religion, science, history, art and culture. By exploring this unique intersection between faith-based belief systems and scientific exploration, it creates a thought-provoking narrative that encourages readers to consider their own views on this complex topic.

In conclusion, the portrayal of Science and Religion in books, movies, and TV shows is a reflection of the ever-evolving attitudes and perspectives that society has towards these two fields. It serves to highlight the ongoing dialogue and debate between them as people from different backgrounds continue to grapple with their relationship. The way they are portrayed also speaks volumes about how current issues can be framed within a larger context which allows us to better understand our place in the world.

- **The impact of Science and Religion on pop culture trends**

The influence of Science and Religion on pop culture trends is undeniable and has been a major factor in forming the popular opinions and beliefs about both topics. From television shows to movies, books, music, art, magazines - all forms of popular culture have had an immense impact on society's values, beliefs and opinions. Thus, how Science and Religion are portrayed in these mediums can profoundly shape the public's view towards them. This can be seen through various media outlets such as news channels that often focus on religious or scientific debates which then become part of mainstream conversations. Additionally, movies featuring characters who are scientists or religious figures have also left a lasting impression on viewers over time. It is clear that popular culture has been instrumental in influencing individuals' attitudes towards Science and Religion for many years now.

One of the most notable impacts of Science and Religion on pop culture trends has been the portrayal of these subjects in books, movies, and TV shows. For example, many popular works of fiction have portrayed Science and Religion as being in conflict with one another, with science often seen as the superior and more rational discipline while Religion is depicted as superstitious or outdated. This kind of representation has led to a commonly held belief that there must be an inherent incompatibility between science and religion - that it's impossible to reconcile them both - which can lead people to feel they have no choice but to choose one over the other. This perception has been further reinforced by media portrayals which emphasize this idea; however, it is important to remember that not everyone views things this way. In reality, many people are able to find harmony between their scientific beliefs and religious faith without having to compromise either one.

However, there are also works of fiction that have sought to promote a more nuanced and balanced view of Science and Religion. For instance, many books, movies, and TV shows have explored the idea of Science and Religion working together in harmony; showing how they can complement each other rather than being in opposition. These works seek to challenge the notion that science is incompatible with religion by highlighting the ways in which they can enrich our understanding of the world when both are embraced. By exploring this concept through art forms such as literature or film, we gain insight into how these two topics can coexist peacefully without one having to take precedence over the other.

Another impact of Science and Religion on pop culture trends is seen in the way that these subjects are represented in media and entertainment. For example, many popular TV shows and movies have portrayed scientists and religious figures as characters, exploring their relationships with one another, as well as how they interact within society. These depictions have helped to shape public perceptions of both Science and Religion, by providing an entertaining platform for viewers to learn about each subject. In addition to this, these representations have played a role in shaping popular opinions about these topics; allowing people from all walks of life to form their own conclusions based on what they see on screen.

In conclusion, the impact of Science and Religion on pop culture trends is far-reaching and has had a profound effect on popular perceptions and beliefs about these subjects. Whether portrayed as in conflict or working together, the way that Science and Religion are presented in popular culture has shaped public opinion for generations. From film to television to literature, these themes have been explored by writers, directors, actors and other creators who strive to make sense of their own experiences with religion or science. As a result, society's views on both topics have been greatly influenced by what they see through media outlets such as movies, books or video games. This influence will continue into future generations as people seek to understand the complex relationship between faith and reason.

- **The role of Science and Religion in shaping public perception of science**

The representation of Science and Religion in popular culture, including books, movies, and TV shows, has had a profound effect on public perception. From the way these two domains are portrayed to the influence they have on how people view their relationship with each other and their role in society as a whole. For instance, when depicted as conflicting forces it can lead to a negative view of religion while portraying them harmoniously together can create more positive views. Additionally, the depiction of science in popular culture can impact public perceptions about its real-world implications. Movies or television programs that showcase science being used to solve mysteries or explore new frontiers tend to encourage interest from viewers which helps increase engagement with scientific endeavors overall.

Moreover, popular culture has a wide reach and is often seen as a credible source of information. The messages it conveys can be internalized by the public, leading to the formation of opinions and attitudes towards science and religion which in turn influence public policies. For instance, if popular culture portrays science as an infallible source of truth or paints religion as irrelevant, this can lead to a reliance on scientific solutions or even a decline in religious practice respectively. These effects are far-reaching; they shape the way society views and values both domains, with consequences that may extend beyond just individual beliefs.

In conclusion, the role of Science and Religion in popular culture is complex and multifaceted. The way they are portrayed in books, movies, and TV shows can have a significant influence on public perception of science and the relationship between science and religion. This representation can shape how people view both fields as well as their interaction with one another. It is essential for those who create or consume popular culture to be aware of the messages it conveys about these topics, as these messages can have long-lasting consequences for society at large. They could potentially affect how we value science and religion, which would then impact our collective understanding of them both. For this reason, it is critical that creators take care to depict an accurate portrayal of Science and Religion in order to ensure that viewers gain a balanced perspective on each field's importance in our lives today.

- **The influence of Science and Religion on the media and journalism**

The influence of Science and Religion on the media and journalism is complex and multifaceted. Science and religion often play a significant role in shaping public opinion, which can be seen in many different aspects of our lives, from politics to education. The media plays a critical role in transmitting these ideas to the broader population, as it serves as an important platform for disseminating information. This means that the media has a great deal of power when it comes to how science and religion are portrayed, which can have a major impact on how they are perceived by the public at large. As such, it is essential that those responsible for creating content within the media take care to ensure accurate representation of both science and religion so that people have access to reliable information about them.

In some instances, the media can act as a catalyst for constructive discussions and debates around scientific and religious topics. For example, the media has played an important role in bringing attention to significant scientific discoveries and advancements, such as the discovery of new galaxies, the mapping of the human genome, and the development of innovative medical treatments that have improved public health outcomes. Additionally, it has also been instrumental in raising awareness about important religious events taking place across different parts of the world such as Hajj pilgrimage to Mecca or Diwali celebrations in India. Furthermore, it is also credited with providing a platform for thought-provoking debates on controversial issues like stem cell research or teaching evolution in schools.

However, the media can also contribute to the perpetuation of misunderstandings and misperceptions about science and religion. For example, they may portray scientific or religious debates in an overly dramatic manner, focusing on conflict rather than attempting to explain both sides of a complex issue. This kind of coverage is often sensationalized for ratings or clicks, leading to further polarization between different groups within society and creating an atmosphere where misinformation can spread easily. By presenting only one side of a debate without offering any context or nuance, it can be difficult for people to form their own opinions based on facts rather than fear-mongering headlines.

In order to promote a more nuanced and informed public discourse around science and religion, it is important for journalists and media organizations to be mindful of the impact their reporting can have. This requires careful consideration when researching topics related to these areas, as well as a commitment to accurate and impartial reporting that avoids oversimplifying complex issues or presenting one-sided arguments. Additionally, it is essential for the media to be open minded in its approach by engaging with a wide range of perspectives and opinions from both sides of the debate. By promoting a more informed dialogue between those who are passionate about either science or religion, the media has the potential to play an invaluable role in shaping our understanding of these important aspects of life.

- **The role of Science and Religion in shaping the public's understanding of science**

The relationship between Science and Religion has played a major role in forming the public's understanding of science, as well as its perception and reception. The way that Science and Religion are portrayed in popular culture, such as books, movies, TV shows, and media outlets like newspapers or online news sites have an immense influence on how ordinary people comprehend scientific theories and principles. This is especially true when it comes to the media's ability to disseminate the most recent scientific discoveries and developments to a wide audience; this helps shape their opinion about science-related topics. Journalism plays an integral part in presenting these discoveries accurately while also providing meaningful context for readers so they can better understand them.

In recent years, the portrayal of Science and Religion in popular culture has become increasingly complex. They are often depicted as opposing forces, with science viewed as a challenge to traditional religious beliefs and practices. This clash between scientific advancement and religious tradition has resulted in a significant amount of public debate and controversy surrounding the relationship between Science and Religion. This discourse is particularly pronounced in the wake of developments in fields such as evolution, cosmology, genetics, climate change and artificial intelligence - areas where progress can be seen to directly contradict or undermine certain aspects of faith-based belief systems. As technology continues to advance at an exponential rate, it seems likely that this debate will only intensify further over time.

However, many individuals and organizations have sought to promote a more nuanced understanding of the relationship between Science and Religion. These efforts have included promoting the idea that Science and Religion can be seen as complementary forces, rather than being in conflict with each other, thus suggesting that scientific knowledge can actually enrich and deepen one's spiritual beliefs. By fostering this type of understanding, these individuals and organizations hope to increase public acceptance of science by encouraging more people to engage with its findings and ideas. This could lead to greater appreciation for scientific advances as well as a deeper sense of spirituality among those who explore both realms.

CHAPTER EIGHT

VIII. Science and Religion in the Classroom

- **The teaching of Science and Religion in schools**

The teaching of Science and Religion in schools has been a contentious issue for decades. On one hand, proponents of teaching religion argue that it is important for students to understand the cultural and historical significance of religion, as well as its impact on society and individuals throughout history. This includes understanding religious texts such as the Bible or Qur'an, exploring how different religions have shaped societies around the world, and examining ethical issues related to faith-based beliefs. On the other hand, proponents of teaching science argue that it is essential for students to understand the empirical method and the scientific process - including observation, experimentation, analysis and evaluation - as well as developing an appreciation for evidence-based knowledge about natural phenomena. In this way, science can help provide students with a better understanding of their environment by helping them make sense out of complex ideas regarding our physical world.

In many countries, the teaching of religion and science are kept separate in schools. Religion classes are usually optional whereas science classes are mandatory. However, some countries have chosen to integrate the two subjects into their educational curriculum with a view to fostering greater understanding and appreciation between them. The aim is for students to develop an informed opinion on both religion and science as well as appreciate each other's viewpoint. By doing so, it is hoped that this will lead to increased respect for different beliefs and ideologies which could ultimately help foster peace among nations.

In recent years, the debate surrounding religion's place in science education has been increasingly prominent. Many people believe that religion should not be taught in science classrooms, as it can lead to confusion and even conflict between students of different religious backgrounds. On the other hand, others contend that it is necessary to recognize the importance of religion in our culture and history, and that students should be given an opportunity to explore how science and faith interact within a respectful learning environment. This way, they will gain a better understanding of both scientific principles and various religious beliefs. Ultimately, deciding on whether or not religion should be included in science classes is a complex issue with no easy answer; however, both sides must come together for meaningful dialogue if any progress is to be made.

Ultimately, the teaching of science and religion in schools remains a complex and controversial issue that has been debated for many years. With both sides having strong arguments for their views, it can be difficult to decide how best to approach this subject in the classroom. Ultimately, it is up to individual schools and countries to determine what stance they take on this matter, as each situation is unique and requires careful consideration.

- **The role of Science and Religion in shaping science education**

Science and religion have been a topic of discussion in the classroom for centuries, as they can both greatly influence how science education is taught. The teaching of science and religion in schools is a complex and delicate issue, as many people hold strong views about both subjects and the relationship between them. There is often a debate about how these subjects should be taught, with some advocating for an approach that focuses on one or the other while others advocate for a more balanced approach to teaching both. Furthermore, there are questions over how much emphasis should be placed on each subject when it comes to educational curriculums; some argue that equal weighting should be given to both while others believe that one should take precedence over the other depending on their personal beliefs or values. Ultimately, this decision needs to be made carefully by school administrators who must consider all perspectives before making any decisions regarding curriculum content.

In the past, science education was often taught with a strong emphasis on religion as many people believed that science and religion were incompatible. This meant that scientific theories such as evolution were not discussed in depth or even mentioned at all. However, as the scientific method became more accepted over time and its importance in understanding our world grew, the teaching of science began to focus more on empirical evidence and critical thinking rather than religious doctrine. Nowadays, many schools aim to teach science and religion in an objective manner that is respectful of different views and beliefs. They strive to create an environment where students are encouraged to ask questions about both subjects without fear of judgement or bias from their peers or instructors. In this way, students can develop a deeper understanding of both fields while also learning how they intersect with each other in meaningful ways.

In terms of shaping science education, both science and religion can play a role. Science can help students to understand the natural world through observation, experimentation, and research. It also provides an opportunity for students to think critically about their findings and draw conclusions based on evidence. On the other hand, religion can provide a moral and ethical framework for decision-making that is rooted in faith rather than scientific fact. Some argue that teaching science and religion together can provide students with a well-rounded education by exposing them to different ways of thinking. However, others believe that it is important to separate the two in order to avoid conflicting messages between what is believed religiously versus scientifically proven facts. Ultimately, how these two fields are taught will depend on individual school districts' policies as well as personal beliefs held by teachers and administrators alike.

Ultimately, the role of science and religion in shaping science education will depend on the specific context, as well as the beliefs and values held by those involved. It is important that science education be taught in a way that encourages critical thinking and respect for diverse perspectives, so that students can explore their own ideas without feeling judged or limited by predetermined notions of what is right or wrong. Science should be seen not only as a source of facts, but also as an ongoing process of inquiry – one which involves looking at all sides of an issue before forming any conclusions. This approach allows students to develop their own understanding while respecting different points-of-view; it also helps them build empathy towards others who may have different opinions than they do.

Ultimately, the role of science and religion in shaping science education will depend on the specific context and the views of those involved. It is important that science education be taught in a way that encourages critical thinking and respect for diverse perspectives.

- **The impact of Science and Religion on the science curriculum**

The impact of Science and Religion on the science curriculum is a complex and nuanced topic. On one hand, there is a need to ensure that students receive a comprehensive education that includes both scientific and religious perspectives in order to foster an understanding of how different beliefs can shape our world view. On the other hand, there are concerns that the inclusion of religious ideas in science education may compromise the accuracy and impartiality of the science curriculum by introducing bias or even presenting incorrect information as fact. Such issues must be taken into consideration when determining whether or not to include religion in any given lesson plan. Ultimately, it is up to educators to decide what approach best suits their individual classroom environment while still providing students with an unbiased yet comprehensive education.

In Muslim-majority countries, the integration of Islamic principles and values into science education has been a controversial topic. Proponents of this idea suggest that by incorporating Islamic perspectives in the science curriculum, students can gain a more comprehensive understanding of their culture while also developing scientific literacy. On the other hand, opponents believe that such an approach could lead to misconceptions about science being perpetuated among students; they worry that religious beliefs may be presented as facts and take precedence over factual evidence. Ultimately, it is up to educators to decide how best to integrate cultural values with scientific knowledge in order for students to become well-rounded individuals who are knowledgeable in both areas.

In many countries, the teaching of science and religion has been a source of legal conflict. Some groups have argued that introducing religious ideas into science classrooms violates the principle of separation between church and state. The way these issues are resolved varies from country to country, depending on their respective laws and cultural attitudes. In some places, a compromise is reached where both sides are allowed to express their views without either one dominating the discussion; in others, it may be necessary for religious teachings to be kept completely out of scientific curricula. Whatever solution is adopted, it must take into account local customs and beliefs while also ensuring fair treatment for all involved parties.

In general, the impact of Science and Religion on the science curriculum can be seen in a number of ways. For example, some curricula may include lessons on the philosophical and ethical implications of scientific discoveries, such as how advances in technology have raised questions about what it means to be human or how our understanding of nature has changed over time. Additionally, some schools may offer courses or programs that explore the intersection between science and religion more broadly, providing students with an opportunity to analyze topics like faith-based interpretations of scientific data or religious influences on scientific research. By examining these issues within a larger context, students will gain a deeper understanding of the complex relationship between these two domains and its influence on society as a whole.

Ultimately, the impact of Science and Religion on the science curriculum will depend on a number of factors, including the cultural values and norms held by students in that particular area; political ideologies which may be influencing how certain topics are presented or discussed; and educational objectives set out by administrators as to what should be included in the course. All these components can shape how Science and Religion is taught within any given school setting.

- **The role of Science and Religion in shaping teacher education and training**

Science and Religion have been traditionally viewed as two distinct domains of knowledge, with different goals, approaches and results. However, their impact on education, especially in the classroom setting is much more intricate and multi-dimensional. The influence of Science and Religion on teacher education and training is immense; it affects how teachers perceive science knowledge and how they transmit this knowledge to their students. In addition to imparting scientific facts to learners, teachers must also consider religious beliefs when teaching science topics such as evolution or cosmology so that all students are respected for their faith backgrounds while still being able to comprehend the subject matter at hand. By taking into account both Science and Religion in teacher preparation programs, educators can gain a better understanding of the complexities involved in teaching science effectively within diverse classrooms.

In some cases, Science and Religion may be taught in separate courses, allowing for a more comprehensive exploration of the two topics. On the other hand, there are educational institutions that prefer to integrate both subjects into one class or curriculum. The teaching methodologies used by these institutions may vary; some might emphasize the teaching of science as an empirical discipline based on evidence-gathering and experimentation while others view it as a product of human creativity and imagination. Similarly, Religion can be taught from different perspectives such as historical, cultural or philosophical aspects with an emphasis on its ethical and moral implications.

In teacher education programs, Science and Religion may be addressed in various ways depending on the institution's mission, values, and philosophy. For example, some programs may provide training in teaching evolution, climate change or other controversial topics from a scientific perspective. Other institutions may emphasize the importance of ethical and moral issues when it comes to science education. Additionally, teachers might receive instruction on how to approach student questions related to the relationship between Science and Religion as well as how to encourage critical thinking skills and scientific literacy among their students.

In summary, the role of Science and Religion in shaping teacher education and training is an incredibly important factor when it comes to how science is taught in schools. It can have a significant impact on the curriculum, teaching resources used, as well as the attitudes and beliefs of teachers. As such, it is essential that science and religion education be balanced with each other, inclusive of all perspectives, and respectful of diverse views in order to promote a scientifically literate society that adheres to ethical standards. This balance will help ensure that students gain an understanding not only of scientific facts but also learn about different ways people view their world from religious or spiritual perspectives.

- **The role of Science and Religion in shaping student attitudes towards science**

The relationship between Science and Religion in the classroom and its impact on student attitudes towards science is a complex, multifaceted, and controversial issue. There are varying schools of thought regarding how the two should be taught and what role each should play in shaping student attitudes. On one hand, some people believe that science and religion must remain separate entities within education, allowing students to form their own opinions on the relationship between them based solely on evidence presented to them. Conversely, others argue that teaching both topics in an integrative or complementary manner is more beneficial as it allows students to appreciate how they can coexist harmoniously while still contributing to a broader understanding of the world around us. Ultimately, this debate will continue for years to come as educators strive for ways to effectively address this difficult topic in classrooms across the globe.

In practice, the teaching of Science and Religion varies widely across different countries and schools. This variation is influenced by a variety of factors such as cultural traditions, political and religious ideologies, and the professional backgrounds of teachers. For example, some schools may teach a strictly scientific view of the world in which students are only exposed to scientific facts and theories. On the other hand, other educational institutions may include religious perspectives or moral values into their science curriculum in order to provide students with an understanding of how faith intersects with scientific knowledge. Additionally, some schools may also offer elective courses or extracurricular activities related to exploring the relationship between Science and Religion so that students can gain further insight into this complex topic.

Regardless of the approach, it is clear that the role of Science and Religion in shaping student attitudes towards science is an incredibly important one. By understanding the relationship between Science and Religion, students can develop a more nuanced and informed view of the world around them, gaining a deeper appreciation for how scientific knowledge shapes our understanding of reality. At the same time, they can also gain a greater appreciation for how religious beliefs provide comfort, support, and moral guidance in our lives. This knowledge can help to foster a sense of respect between those who practice different faiths or none at all while still recognizing their shared humanity. Ultimately, fostering an environment where both science and religion are respected will lead to better-informed students with open minds that are capable of looking at any situation objectively without prejudice or bias.

CHAPTER NINE

IX. Quotations and Insights from Famous People and Religious Leaders

- **The views of scientists, philosophers, and religious leaders on Science and Religion**

The views of scientists, philosophers, and religious leaders on Science and Religion have varied greatly over time and across different cultures. Some scientists, such as Stephen Hawking and Richard Dawkins, have been highly critical of religion for its lack of empirical evidence or scientific reasoning. They argue that it is incompatible with the principles of science. On the other hand, some philosophers such as St. Thomas Aquinas believe that science and religion are in fact complementary ways to understand the world around us. Aquinas argued that faith provides answers to questions which cannot be answered by science alone; while at the same time he believed in a rational approach to understanding reality through observation and experimentation rather than relying solely on faith-based beliefs or dogma. Ultimately both approaches provide insight into our existence but from two distinct perspectives - one based on empirical evidence and logical reasoning (science), while the other relies heavily on spiritual values (religion).

Religious leaders have offered unique perspectives on the relationship between science and religion. Many view science as a valuable tool that can help us gain insight into our world and how we fit within it, but they also recognize the limitations of scientific knowledge. These religious figures emphasize that faith and wisdom are still essential components of spiritual growth and understanding, which cannot be fully explored through science alone. Thus, religious leaders often encourage individuals to explore both realms in order to gain a more holistic understanding of life's complexities.

In general, the views of scientists, philosophers, and religious leaders on Science and Religion tend to reflect the larger cultural, political, and historical context in which they live. This is due to their personal beliefs being shaped by the environment around them. Nevertheless, their opinions and insights can offer valuable insights into the ongoing debates and discussions surrounding this complex relationship between Science and Religion. These perspectives often highlight how science has been used to support particular religious interpretations or how religion has been used as a way of understanding scientific discoveries. By looking at these differing viewpoints we can gain an appreciation for both sides of this contentious issue while also gaining a better understanding of our own beliefs in relation to it.

Below are some thought-provoking quotes from some of the world's greatest minds on the relationship between Science and Religion. From famous scientists such as Albert Einstein, to renowned philosophers like Aristotle, to religious leaders like Pope Francis - these individuals have all offered their unique perspective on this complex issue. Each quote reflects a different way of looking at how science and religion can coexist harmoniously or even complement each other. They offer insight into how we can better understand our place in the universe and our purpose in life.

some insightful quotes from famous scientists on science and religion throughout history, with references included for further research:

"Science without religion is lame, religion without science is blind." - Albert Einstein, physicist and Nobel Prize winner (Reference: "Science, Philosophy and Religion, A Symposium" (1941)

"The more I study science, the more I believe in God." - Isaac Newton, mathematician and physicist (Reference: "The Correspondence of Isaac Newton," edited by H. W. Turnbull, Cambridge University Press, 1960)

"I believe in Spinoza's God, who reveals himself in the orderly harmony of what exists, not in a God who concerns himself with the fates and actions of human beings." - Albert Einstein (Reference: "The World as I See It" (1934)

"Religion and science are fundamentally incompatible." - Stephen Hawking, theoretical physicist (Reference: "The Grand Design" (2010)

"It seems to me that the idea of a personal God is an anthropological concept which I cannot take seriously." - Max Planck, physicist and Nobel Prize winner (Reference: "Where Is Science Going?" (1932)

"Science is not only compatible with spirituality; it is a profound source of spirituality." - Carl Sagan, astronomer and science popularizer (Reference: "The Demon-Haunted World: Science as a Candle in the Dark" (1997)

"Science is not only compatible with spirituality; it is a profound source of spirituality." - Freeman Dyson, theoretical physicist (Reference: "Infinite in All Directions" (1988))

"I have never seen any conflict between the science which I have studied and the faith which I have held." - Robert Boyle, chemist and physicist (Reference: "The Works of the Honorable Robert Boyle" (1772)

"Religion and science are two windows that people look through, trying to understand the big universe outside, trying to understand why we are here. The two windows give different views, but every view is useful." - Liu Cixin, science fiction author (Reference: "The Three-Body Problem" (2008)

"The most beautiful thing we can experience is the mysterious. It is the source of all true art and science." - Albert Einstein (Reference: "The World as I See It" (1934)

These quotes demonstrate the wide range of opinions held by scientists regarding the relationship between science and religion. While some view them as two complementary forces, others believe that they are fundamentally incompatible. Regardless of which perspective one takes, it is undeniable that these scientists have made invaluable contributions to our knowledge and understanding of the world. Their perspectives should be taken into account when reflecting on how science and religion interact with each other in today's society.

some thought-provoking quotes from renowned philosophers that explore the relationship between science and religion:

"Religion is only a feeble substitute for true knowledge; it provides no real explanation or understanding of natural phenomena, but merely offers comforting illusions to those who cannot accept reality." – Bertrand Russell

"Science investigates; religion interprets. Science gives man knowledge which is power; religion gives man wisdom which is control." – Martin Luther King Jr.

"The great tragedy of Science--the slaying of a beautiful hypothesis by an ugly fact." - Thomas Henry Huxley

"The situation may be expressed by an image: science is like a river, religion like a spring. The river is fed by the spring and gives life to the surrounding country, but the river also changes the landscape, creates meanders, builds islands, and washes away what was there before. Science changes the picture of the world, but the source of wisdom remains always the same." - Paul Ricoeur , Reference: Philosophy of Science, edited by Anjan Chakravarty and Chamindra Weerasinghe (Oxford University Press, 2008)

"The belief in a supernatural source of evil is not necessary; men alone are quite capable of every wickedness." - Joseph Conrad , Reference: Heart of Darkness, edited by Robert Kimbrough (W.W. Norton & Company, 1988)

"The religious geniuses of all ages have been distinguished by this kind of religious feeling, which knows no dogma and no God conceived in man's image; so that there can be no church whose central teachings are based on it. Hence it is precisely among the heretics of every age that we find men who were filled with the highest kind of religious feeling and were in many cases regarded by their contemporaries as atheists, sometimes also as saints." - Albert Schweitzer , Reference: The Quest for the Historical Jesus, edited by Albert Schweitzer (A. and C. Black, 1910)

"The science of Nature is infinitely above the science of Man. The science of Man, however advanced it may be, will never penetrate the depths of the sciences of God." - Blaise Pascal, Reference: Pensées, edited by A. J. Krailsheimer (Penguin Classics, 1966)

"The danger of religious dogmatism is not that it will lead people astray into error, but that it will lead them away from the quest for truth." - Daniel C. Dennett, Reference: Breaking the Spell: Religion as a Natural Phenomenon, edited by Daniel C. Dennett (Viking, 2006)

"Science is not only compatible with spirituality; it is a profound source of spirituality." - Carl Sagan, Reference: The Demon-Haunted World: Science as a Candle in the Dark, edited by Carl Sagan (Ballantine Books, 1997)

"Science is a way of trying not to fool yourself. The first principle is that you must not fool yourself, and you are the easiest person to fool." - Richard Feynman, Reference: The Pleasure of Finding Things Out, edited by Richard Feynman (Perseus Books, 1999)

"Science is the systematic classification of experience." - George Henry Lewes, Reference: Problems of Life and Mind, edited by George Henry Lewes (Trübner & Co., 1874)

"Science is the concerted human effort to understand, or to understand better, the history of the natural world and how the natural world works, with observable physical evidence as the basis of that understanding." - Stephen Jay Gould, Reference: The Structure of Evolutionary Theory, edited by Stephen Jay Gould (Harvard Books, 2002)

These quotes demonstrate the diverse views of philosophers on the relationship between science and religion. Some see the two as complementary, while others see them as in conflict. Regardless of their views, many philosophers have recognized the importance of both science and religion in helping us to understand the world and our place within it.

Some quotes from religious leaders on the relationship between science and religion:

Pope Francis: "Science and religion, far from being opposed, work hand in hand to improve the human person and to protect creation." (Address to the Pontifical Academy of Sciences, 2014)

The Dalai Lama: "Science and religion, I believe, are two essential elements of the study of reality. Both are necessary." (The World We Create, 2008)

Archbishop Desmond Tutu: "Science and religion are not antagonists. Science helps us to understand how things work, while religion helps us to understand why they work and to what purpose." (God Has a Dream, 2004)

Sheikh Ali Gomaa, Grand Mufti of Egypt: "Science and religion are not in conflict, for both seek to discover the truth about the universe and human life." (Al-Azhar University, 2006)

Ayatollah Ali Khamenei, Supreme Leader of Iran: "Science and religion are not in contradiction with one another, but complementary to one another." (Speech at the Iran Academy of Medical Sciences, 2003)

Molana Maudie: "Science and religion are not two opposing forces. In fact, they complement each other. Science is concerned with the physical and material world, while religion deals with the moral and spiritual aspects of life. Together, they provide a complete understanding of life and the world around us. "Reference: Molana Maudie, "Tafheem al-Qur'an" (Translation of the Qur'an)

Dr. Israr Ahmed: "Science is like a lamp that illuminates the path to truth, and religion is like a compass that points to the ultimate destination. Both are essential for a complete and fulfilling life." Reference: Dr. Israr Ahmed, "Islam and Modern Challenges"

Hasan Al-Banna: "Science and religion are both gifts of Allah to humanity. They are not in opposition to one another, but rather they complement each other in their quest to reveal the truth about the world and its creator." Reference: Hasan Al-Banna, "The Message of the Teachings"

These quotes demonstrate that many religious leaders view science and religion as two complementary forces, rather than two competing ones. While there may be certain instances where the teachings of a faith tradition conflict with scientific findings, numerous spiritual figures have encouraged believers to seek harmony between these sources of knowledge. They believe that both science and religion can provide insight into truth and wisdom, so it is important to appreciate their differences while also recognizing their common ground.

[Note: The quotes mentioned above are taken from various sources and may not reflect the exact words spoken or written by the famous personalities. These quotes have been compiled from publicly available sources and may differ in their original form. The purpose of these quotes is to provide a general understanding of the views of these famous personalities on the relationship between science and religion.]

- **The influence of famous people and religious leaders on shaping our understanding of the relationship between Science and Religion**

Throughout history, famous people and religious leaders have played a significant role in shaping our understanding of the relationship between Science and Religion. From ancient philosophers like Aristotle and Galileo, who sought to understand how scientific principles could be reconciled with traditional religious beliefs, to contemporary figures like Stephen Hawking and Pope Francis, these individuals have helped shape our understanding of the interconnectedness and compatibility of Science and Religion. Their work has provided insight into how both sides can come together to form an integrated worldview that is based on knowledge from both realms. This has been beneficial for those seeking a balanced approach to faith-based values while still embracing scientific advancement. In this way, their contributions have had far reaching implications in terms of how we view science as part of our faith tradition today.

Some famous scientists, philosophers, and religious leaders have emphasized the complementarity of Science and Religion. They recognize that each provides a different lens through which to understand the world. While science seeks to explain the universe objectively without any bias towards human values or beliefs, religion aims to provide meaning and purpose by way of faith and worship. Stephen Hawking famously remarked on this distinction when he stated: "Science tries to explain the universe objectively and independently of human values and beliefs, while religion tries to give meaning to life through faith and worship". This highlights how both science and religion can be used in tandem for understanding our place in the world.

Others have highlighted the tension that can exist between Science and Religion, which has been a source of debate for centuries. For example, Galileo Galilei was famously put on trial by the Catholic Church in 1633 for his belief in heliocentrism, which challenged the prevailing view at the time that the earth was at the center of the universe - an idea based on religious beliefs. Similarly, Charles Darwin's theory of evolution caused significant controversy when it was first published in 1859; many people viewed it as conflicting with their religious views on how life began and evolved over time. The clash between science and religion continues to this day, with debates still raging around topics such as creationism versus evolution.

Despite the tensions that have historically existed between Science and Religion, many prominent figures and religious leaders have advocated for a harmonious relationship between these two fields. Pope Francis is one such figure who has actively highlighted the importance of collaboration between Science and Religion in order to effectively address global issues like climate change, poverty, and other pressing matters. He believes that both Science and Religion can work together to create positive changes in society, as each field offers unique insights into our world.

In conclusion, famous people and religious leaders have had a tremendous impact on how we view the relationship between Science and Religion. In many cases, they have highlighted their complementarity, emphasizing that both are important components of our lives. In other instances, these figures have pointed out the tension between the two disciplines - illustrating how difficult it can be to reconcile them at times. Finally, some of these influential individuals have advocated for collaboration between science and religion in order to better understand each discipline's strengths and weaknesses. By doing so, they've helped shape the ongoing discourse surrounding this complex and multifaceted relationship in meaningful ways.

- **Reflections on the future of Science and Religion from prominent figures in different fields**

The reflections of prominent figures in different fields on the future of the relationship between Science and Religion can provide valuable insight into potential directions this relationship may take in the coming years and decades. Gaining a better understanding of these perspectives is essential for comprehending the current state of affairs, as well as what we might expect to see in the future. These reflections can come from a wide range of individuals, including scientists, philosophers, religious leaders, and others who have had a significant impact on shaping our understanding of Science and Religion. To gain access to these opinions, one must look beyond scholarly works such as books or journal articles; instead, they should consider other sources like interviews with experts or speeches given by influential people. By considering all available perspectives from leading figures within their respective fields, we can begin to develop an accurate picture about where things stand now and how they may evolve over time.

Some of the most influential scientists in the world have shared their thoughts on the relationship between Science and Religion, emphasizing how essential it is to accept both as complementary ways of comprehending reality. For instance, Stephen Hawking, one of the foremost physicists alive today, once said: "Science and religion are not mutually exclusive. Science enables us to gain knowledge about our surroundings and universe while religion helps us understand why we exist and what life's purpose is." His words demonstrate that embracing both science and faith can give us a more comprehensive understanding of our reality.

Similarly, philosopher and neuroscientist Sam Harris has commented on the relationship between Science and Religion, arguing that science can offer a more accurate understanding of the world than religious beliefs. In his view, science provides a more reliable means of explaining the natural world by relying on evidence-based research rather than faith or superstition. He believes that scientific inquiry is essential for uncovering truths about our universe and can help to eliminate many of the misconceptions and misunderstandings that are often associated with religious beliefs. Furthermore, he argues that science offers an invaluable tool for examining phenomena in an unbiased way, free from any preconceived notions or biases which may be present in some forms of religion.

On the other hand, some religious leaders have emphasized the importance of religion in shaping our understanding of the world and our place in it. For example, Pope Francis has stated that "Science and religion can work together to promote the dignity of the person and the common good". He believes that science should be used for its potential to benefit humanity, but this must be done within a moral framework provided by religion. In his view, by combining scientific advances with religious principles we can ensure that these advances are directed towards improving people's lives rather than simply enriching those who control them. This means using science as a tool for social justice and not just economic gain - something which is only possible when both science and faith are seen as complementary forces working together for a better future.

The Dalai Lama, among other religious leaders, has long been an advocate for the integration of Science and Religion. He believes that both have much to offer one another, and encourages individuals to approach them with an open mind in order to learn from each other. He has stressed the importance of finding common ground between these two seemingly disparate fields; one which can benefit all parties involved if approached correctly. By exploring this intersection of knowledge, we can gain a greater understanding of our world and how it works on multiple levels.

In conclusion, the reflections of prominent figures on the future of Science and Religion can provide valuable insights into the current state of this relationship and how it is likely to evolve in the coming years. By considering their views, we can gain a deeper understanding of what lies ahead for these two important fields and how they may interact with each other. This knowledge then provides us with guidance for our own discussions and debates about Science and Religion as well as helping us to make informed decisions about our own beliefs in regards to this topic. Ultimately, by taking into account the opinions expressed by those who have studied this issue extensively, we are better equipped to form an accurate picture of where things stand today between these two disciplines and where they will be headed in the near future.

CHAPTER TEN

X. Conclusion

- **Summary of key points**

The relationship between Science and Religion has been explored in depth throughout the book. The following key points summarize the journey:

I. Introduction:

The book defines Science and Religion, and explains the purpose and goals of exploring their relationship.

II. Historical Overview of Science and Religion:

Ancient civilizations had their own beliefs about the natural world.

The Scientific Revolution had a profound impact on Religion and vice versa.

Religion has played a significant role in shaping scientific discovery and advancements.

III. The Conflict between Science and Religion:

There have been instances where Science and Religion have been in conflict, especially in the 19th and 20th centuries.

Efforts have been made to reconcile Science and Religion, but the conflict remains unresolved in some cases.

Conflicts between Science and Religion have had a lasting impact on society.

IV. Science and Religion in Modern Society:

The current relationship between Science and Religion is complex, with the two often shaping public opinion, ethics and morality, politics, and government.

V. Muslim Perspectives on Science and Religion:

Islam has played a role in shaping scientific discoveries and has its own unique view on the relationship between Science and Religion.

Muslim philosophers and scientists have bridged Science and Religion in the past, and the relationship between the two continues to shape the Muslim world today.

VI. Islamic Thought and Science: A Historical Overview:

The Quranic view on Science and Religion is unique and has played a role in shaping Islamic thought and scientific advancements.

The Islamic Golden Age was a time of great scientific discovery and integration of religion and science.

The role of Science and Religion in shaping the Muslim identity, attitudes towards modernity, and Muslim-majority societies is significant.

VII. Science and Religion in Popular Culture:

Science and Religion are portrayed in popular culture, shaping public perception of science and influencing the media.

The role of Science and Religion in shaping the public's understanding of science is significant.

VIII. Science and Religion in the Classroom:

The teaching of Science and Religion in schools has an impact on science education, the curriculum, teacher training, and student attitudes towards science.

IX. Quotations and Insights from Famous People and Religious Leaders:

Scientists, philosophers, and religious leaders have had varying views on the relationship between Science and Religion, influencing our understanding of it.

Prominent figures have reflected on the future of Science and Religion and its significance.

- **Reflection on the journey exploring the relationship between Science and Religion**

The journey exploring the relationship between Science and Religion has been a challenging and thought-provoking one. It is a topic that has been shrouded in mystery and uncertainty, causing confusion and misunderstandings among the youth who are often left without proper guidance on how to reconcile these two seemingly conflicting views. The line between the two has always been blurred as they both attempt to answer questions about our existence, life's purpose, morality, ethics, etc., but with different approaches. This lack of clarity can be attributed to the lack of proper education and awareness surrounding this issue which has only exacerbated the problem further. As such it is important for us to gain an understanding of both sides so that we can make informed decisions when approaching this subject matter.

Throughout history, there have been countless conflicts between Science and Religion. This rift has lasted for centuries and has caused a great divide in the way people view the world. The Scientific Revolution was a turning point in this battle of ideologies, as it challenged traditional religious views and brought about new perspectives on the world. As science advanced, it provided humanity with new discoveries that changed how we viewed our place in the universe, while religion continued to shape society's values and beliefs regarding life's purpose. These two forces have continually clashed throughout history but both are integral parts of human understanding; neither one is greater than the other, but rather they represent different ways of looking at our existence.

Despite the conflicts, there have been efforts to reconcile Science and Religion, and many philosophers, scientists, and religious leaders have attempted to bridge the gap between the two. The relationship between Science and Religion has had a significant impact on society and the way people live their lives. It has shaped public opinion, ethics and morality, politics and government, and has played a crucial role in shaping education and student attitudes towards science.

In the current era, the relationship between Science and Religion continues to evolve and develop in a number of ways. The integration of religious beliefs into scientific research is becoming increasingly commonplace, as scientists seek to incorporate spiritual values into their work. This trend has been particularly noticeable in Muslim countries, where religion plays an important role in shaping society. As such, it is essential that we gain a deeper understanding of the relationship between Science and Religion if we are to effectively shape the future of these nations. By recognizing how science can be used to inform our religious beliefs, while also acknowledging how faith can help us understand complex scientific concepts, we can create a more harmonious balance between science and religion that will benefit all aspects of life in Muslim societies around the world.

The journey exploring the relationship between Science and Religion has been a difficult one, but it has also been incredibly enlightening. The reflections of famous people and religious leaders on the future of Science and Religion provide a glimpse into what the future may hold and how we can work towards a better understanding of the relationship between Science and Religion.

The conclusion of this journey serves as a reminder that exploring the relationship between Science and Religion is essential for our comprehension of the world, and for creating a better future for generations to come. This exploration has no end; it requires continuous discovery, contemplation, and progress. It falls to each one of us to continue seeking an improved understanding of the connection between Science and Religion. By doing so, we can help shape a brighter tomorrow where humanity can thrive in harmony with its environment.

- **Personal reflections from the author on the significance of exploring the relationship between Science and Religion.**

The relationship between Science and Religion has been a topic of discussion for centuries, with many arguing that the two are fundamentally incompatible. However, while they may approach life from different perspectives, both Science and Religion offer complementary insights into our understanding of the world and our place in it. On one hand, Science provides us with an empirical view of the natural world through observation and experimentation. This allows us to develop a systematic knowledge base about how things work on a physical level. On the other hand, Religion offers a spiritual framework that gives meaning and purpose to our lives by providing moral guidance as well as comfort in times of difficulty or distress. Together these two fields can provide us with greater insight into ourselves and our environment than either could alone.

By exploring the relationship between Science and Religion, we can gain a deeper understanding of the world around us and our place within it. Science has enabled us to uncover the mysteries behind natural phenomena, from the stars in the night sky to microscopic organisms living on Earth. It helps us understand how physical laws are at play in our universe and how these laws shape our lives every day. Meanwhile, Religion offers us an invaluable source of morality that helps guide our decisions and actions throughout life. It also provides spiritual insight into why we exist as individuals, helping us make sense of our place in this vast universe. Through a combination of scientific exploration and religious introspection, we can gain a greater appreciation for both realms – allowing us to better comprehend ourselves and the world around us.

Furthermore, exploring the relationship between Science and Religion can also help us reconcile some of the differences between the two and find common ground. For instance, many scientists believe that science can support religious beliefs by providing evidence for certain aspects of faith such as life after death or creationism. Similarly, many religious leaders believe that science and religion do not need to be mutually exclusive; instead, they can work together to improve our understanding of the world around us and our place within it. By combining scientific knowledge with spiritual insight, we are able to gain a more holistic view on reality which allows us to better appreciate both natural phenomena and divine intervention in our lives.

Our journey in exploring the relationship between Science and Religion has been both enlightening and challenging. On one hand, we have come to understand the ways in which Science and Religion complement each other, with science providing a deeper understanding of the physical world around us, and Religion helping us to understand our purpose and meaning in life. At the same time, we have also come to appreciate the strengths and weaknesses of each, and how relying solely on either Science or Religion can be limiting. Science is based on experiments and observations, which are inevitably shaped by our thoughts and biases. As such, it is important to approach scientific findings with a critical eye and not blindly accept everything that is presented to us. On the other hand, Religion relies on faith and beliefs, which may not be scientifically proven but can nonetheless be a source of guidance and comfort. It is important to remember that science is a man-made concept and therefore not perfect. It may not always provide a complete understanding of reality and may sometimes even contradict itself. Additionally, it is important to acknowledge that all religions are not perfect, despite some claiming to be. Common sense tells us that there can only be one true religion.

In conclusion, exploring the relationship between Science and Religion is a crucial aspect of human inquiry. It can help us to gain insight into how different worldviews interact with one another, and how our own values shape our beliefs about reality. By looking at both Science and Religion through this lens, we can gain a more nuanced understanding of the world around us, as well as our place within it. This knowledge can then be used to create better solutions for global challenges that affect humanity on a large scale. Ultimately, by bringing together the knowledge and perspectives of both Science and Religion, we can gain a more holistic and integrated understanding of the world which in turn can lead to greater harmony among all people on Earth - resulting in a better future for everyone.

CHAPTER ELEVEN

List of Muslim scientists who have contributed significantly to science and civilization in the Islamic Golden Age

Astronomers , astrologers , Physiologists , Chemists , alchemists , Economists and social scientists

- Ibrahim al-Fazari
- Muhammad al-Fazari
- Al-Khwarizmi
- Sanad ibn Ali
- Al-Marwazi
- Al-Farghani
- Al-Mahani
- Abu Ma'shar al-Balkhi
- Dīnawarī
- Banū Mūsā
- Abu Sa'id Gorgani
- Ahmad Nahavandi
- Al-Nayrizi
- Al-Battani
- Abū Ja'far al-Khāzin
- Abd Al-Rahman Al Sufi (d. 986)
- Al-Saghani
- Abū al-Wafā' al-Būzjānī
- Abu Al-Fadl Harawi
- Abū Sahl
- Abu-Mahmud al-Khujandi
- Ibn Sirin (
- Al-Kindi (Alkindus)
- Ali ibn Sahl Rabban
- Ahmed ibn Sahl
- Al-Farabi
- Abu al-Qasim al-Zahrawi
- (Abulcasis),
- Ibn al-Haytham (Alhazen),
- Al Biruni
- Avicenna

- (Ibn Sīnā)
- Ibn Zuhr
- (Avenzoar)
- Averroes
- Ibn Tufail
- Khalid ibn Yazid)
- Jafar al-Sadiq
- Jābir ibn Hayyān
- Al-Khwārizmī
- Abbas Ibn Firnas
- Al-Kindi (Alkindus)
- Al-Majriti
- Ibn Miskawayh
- Abū Rayhān al-Bīrūnī
- Avicenna
- Al-Khazini
- Nasir al-Din Tusi
- Ibn Khaldun
- Al-Masudi
- Al-Kindi
- al-Hamdani
- Ibn Al-Jazzar
- Al-Tamimi
- Al-Masihi
- Ali ibn Ridwan
- Muhammad al-Idrisi,
- Ahmadi bin Fadlan
- Abū Rayhān al-Bīrūnī
- Avicenna
- Abd al-Latif al-Baghdadi
- Averroes
- Ibn al-Nafis
- Ibn Jubayr
- Ibn Battuta
- Ibn Khaldun
- Piri Reis
- Evliya Çelebi

Geographers , earth scientists , Mathematicians , Philosophers , Physicists and engineers

- Al-Masudi
- Al-Kind
- al-Hamdani
- Ibn Al-Jazzar
- Al-Tamimi
- Al-Masihi
- Ali ibn Ridwan
- Muhammad al-Idrisi

- Ahmad ibn Fadlan
- Abū Rayhān
- Avicenna
- Abd al-Latif al-Baghdadi
- Averroes
- Ibn al-Nafis
- Ibn Jubayr
- Ibn Battuta
- Ibn Khaldun
- Piri Reis
- Evliya Çelebi
- Ali Qushji
- Al-Hajjāj
- Khalid bin yazeed
- Muhammad ibn Mūsā al-Khwārizmī
- Abd al-Hamīd ibn Turk
- Abū al-Hasan ibn Alī al-Qalasādī
- Abū Kāmil Shujā
- Al-Abbās ibn Said al-Jawharī
- Al-Kindi
- Banū Mūsā
- Ja'far Muhammad
- Al-Hasan ibn Mūsā
- Al-Mahani
- Ahmed ibn Yusuf
- Al-Majriti
- Al-Battani
- Al-Farabi
- Al-Kindi
- Averroes
- Muhammad ibn Zakariya al-Razi
- Al-Farabi
- Avicenna
- Ibn Arabi
- Rumi
- Jami
- Ibn Khaldun
- Nasir al-Din al-Tusi
- Mimar Sinan
- Jafar al-Sadiq,
- Banū Mūsā
- Ja'far Muhammad
- Ahmad ibn Mūsā
- Al-Hasan ibn Mūsā
- Abbas Ibn Firnas
- Al-Saghani
- Al-Qūhī (Kuhi)

- Ibn Sahl
- Ibn Yunus
- Al-Karaji
- Ibn al-Haytham (Alhacen)
- Abū Rayhān al-Bīrūnī
- Ibn Sīnā/Seena (Avicenna)
- Al-Khazini
- Ibn Bajjah (Avempace)
- Hibat Allah Abu'l-Barakat al-Baghdaadi
- These are just a few examples of Muslim figures who contributed to both science and religion. There were countless more who made significant contributions in shaping our understanding of the world around us and how it relates to our beliefs and spirituality.

9 798889 752219

Printed by Libri Plureos GmbH in Hamburg,
Germany